NYMPH FISHING
FOR
LARGER TROUT

Charles E. Brooks

NYMPH FISHING
FOR LARGER TROUT

Illustrated by Dave Whitlock

CROWN PUBLISHERS, INC.   NEW YORK

Manufactured in the United States of America
Published simultaneously in Canada by General
Publishing Company Limited

Designed by Shari de Miskey

Library of Congress Cataloging in Publication Data

Brooks, Charles E.   1921–
    Nymph fishing for larger trout.
    Includes index.
    1. Trout fishing.   2. Fly fishing.   3. Nymphs
(Insects)   I. Title.
SH687.B832   799.1'7'55   76-10159
ISBN: 0-517-525518
10 9 8 7 6 5 4 3 2

Contents

Introduction

NYMPH FISHING HAS ONLY BEEN EXPLORED FOR ABOUT SEVENTY-FIVE YEARS; HOWEVER, it is surprising that, while more study, advancement, and writing on other facets of fly-fishing have been done during this period than in all the rest of its recorded history, there has been not one definitive work on fishing the artificial nymph.

One of the reasons, perhaps the major one, has been the difficulty of obtaining and identifying the nymphs of the streams the angler fishes. I will explain how to overcome some of this difficulty herein, but the problem of identifying the immature form of trout-stream insects will not be solved in the immediate future, if ever. There is no easy method; nor does it appear that one can ever be formulated.

One *must* know what the major nymphs are that inhabit the stream he fishes, and he must know in what water and bottom types the particular insect he wishes to imitate may be found. How to obtain this information is one of my main reasons for writing this book. But this information, even when it is obtained will be of *direct* value only to the angler obtaining it; I know of no way that he can transmit it to anyone else. Perhaps this is another reason for there being no definitive work on the subject: most of the time, the angler *must* obtain his own information firsthand.

Scientific works on nymph identification are almost worthless to the angler, for they are so necessarily technical that he cannot possibly use the information. For example, even the most expert entomologists, in order to identify certain species of mayfly, have to have the genitalia of a *virgin adult male* of the species. And not even the best of them can make a sure identification, in all cases, of the underwater immature form.

You do not need to know the species, or even the genus, of a nymph you have captured in a riffle on your favorite trout stream, in order to tie a good representative artificial of that nymph. But once tied, what are you going to do with it? How does the natural act, where does it live, what are its habits? To answer these questions you have to identify the nymph, and that, sir—or madam—is the problem.

For the past fifteen years I have spent about 85 percent of my fishing time fishing nymphs. For the last ten years I have spent about a hundred days a year on the water, and over half of that has been spent gathering nymphs and information on them.

I have seined thousands of nymphs and collected hundreds for identification. I have exhausted the library resources of two western state universities, and I have read all the fishing books about nymphs that I know of, and still I must tell you that I have been unable to conceive a simple plan for identifying immature trout-stream insects. Far more intelligent, educated, and dedicated men than I have also failed to do so.

Having made this explanation, I hope you will accept this book for what it is: my very best effort to help you find your way into the most productive of all fly-fishing methods for trout, and particularly for larger trout.

CHARLES E. BROOKS
WEST YELLOWSTONE, MONTANA

1 Becoming a Nymph Fisherman

LIKE MOST FLY-FISHERS, I TOOK A LONG TIME BECOMING A NYMPH FISHERMAN. BUT I have a partial excuse: when I began fly-fishing, by way of fly-tying, back in the Missouri Ozarks, I was only nine years old.

In the winter of 1930 I started tying flies and the following spring saw me become a "fly-fisherman" with a seasoned hickory pole, homemade line, and horsehair leaders. Though I read the outdoor magazines assiduously then, especially the fly-fishing portions, I had never heard the word "nymph." It would be over fifteen years before I did.

After World War II, serving as a ranger in Yosemite National Park, I came in touch with better trout streams and more knowledgeable fly-fishermen. Although none of these fellows used the nymph much, some of them carried a few patterns and had enough knowledge to explain some of the facts of underwater life to me. One of these visiting fly-fishermen, from Pennsylvania, used a cased caddis pattern and had great success with it in the Merced around the Arch Rock Ranger Station. This was the first "nymph" pattern I ever saw successfully used: within another year it became the first that I used, and it is still one of my standbys. That Pennsylvania fisherman called cased caddis "periwinkles," and I never hear that word without an instant flashback to that day in the forties when I saw my first trout taken on a "nymph."

A year or so later I was fishing, without success, one of the forks of the Yuba not far from Downieville when I came to a bedrock section. The water was crystal clear, shallow, and the bedrock bottom was covered with large cased caddis. They were actually so thick that by bringing the edges of one's hands along the bottom for a few inches, then cupping them together, one could pick up more than a dozen.

They were about an inch long, as thick as a goose quill, and their cases were made of sand grains and tiny dark pebbles. In those days I always had my fly-tying kit with me, and I went back to the car to tie up some imitations. It was a difficult task—and it still is. I wasn't the only one trying to imitate and fish that particular caddis, I soon found. A number of fellows were working on the idea, but it was a problem which no one has ever actually solved. Some flytiers got so desperate for a good imitation that they resorted to catching the naturals, removing the grub and slipping the sand-pebble case over the hook, stuffing the case full of glue-soaked cotton, then winding on a short black hackle. Others tried winding on an under-sized dark wool body, soaking it in glue, and then rolling it in a pan of fine dark sand. I went the latter route but results were unsatisfactory. No glue then available would hold the pebbles on the wool after the fly was well soaked in water.

When I went to Alaska, three years later, the only nymph pattern I carried was that cased caddis imitation. I had reentered the Air Force, with the intent of adding the necessary seventeen years to the three and a half I already had invested, so that after twenty, I could retire and go trout fishing. My outdoor background and my particular job got me assigned to faraway places where there wasn't much going on but where the fishing was fabulous. During the two years I spent in Alaska, I fished so much that there were times that I felt like a professional fisherman.

This was to prove invaluable; I got completely over ever wanting to catch fish for the sake of catching, and I began to experiment with various methods.

Most of the fish in interior Alaska, except during salmon spawning time, are grayling. One often hears that the Arctic grayling is an easy fish, and when the fish is in a taking mood, this is true: they seem almost determined to be caught. But when they are not in the mood, no more difficult fly fish exists, and I am glad to see that the very experienced and knowledgeable fly-fisherman Roderick Haig-Brown agrees with this conclusion, as he relates in his fine book *Fisherman's Summer.*

An old sourdough, Jack Warren, who lived near Big Delta and worked as an adviser to the Army Survival School, was the first to show me that indisposed grayling could be taken on nymphs. Jack used only three patterns of flies: a green wormlike caddis, which he called Rockworm, that I did not recognize then but know now was a *Rhyacophila* imitation, a black mayfly type, and an indeterminate gray one very similar to the present-day Muskrat Nymph.

This was in the fall of 1951 and it wasn't until winter had set in and fishing was over that I got to thinking that I had made no attempt to find out if those nymphs of Jack's actually imitated any aquatic creatures as he had said.

I was getting a little smarter (though not much) and I was beginning to realize that I actually knew very little about trout and trout streams. I have always been a great reader and lover of books and it came naturally for me to try to solve my problem by finding some books on the subject.

I went to the University of Alaska, a few miles from where I lived in Fairbanks, and looked through their slim supply of books without finding one on Alaskan insects. The librarian put me in touch with a biology professor who laughed at the idea that anyone would waste his time on such a silly subject. Since I had been trying for several years to get a copy of the only book that I knew of that dealt with trout streams—*Trout Streams* by Paul Needham— I was pretty subdued by the professor's report and did not go probing around for books on aquatic insects until several years had passed. The professor had a point; books on aquatic entomology were *very* few at that time and those that were available were either quite general or very limited in scope. However, it was the recognition that I knew so little about underwater life that actually decided my future course of action; I determined that I would begin to learn something about these creatures on my own, although at the time I was unsure how to commence.

I got some help on the problem the following year. I met Sid Gordon on the Yellowstone, doing research for his book *How to Fish from Top to Bottom*. Gordon explained some of the difficulties I would encounter and recommended the works of the Needhams, father and son. He also got me interested in water chemistry and quality, which along with knowledge of nymphs, are abiding interests today.

My road to becoming a knowledgeable and experienced nymph fisherman was rough and bumpy; the student today will find it much easier. My attempt was also complicated by a complete lack of sympathy on the part of the Air Force, which for the next six years shipped me all over the globe, always to the most arid and unlikely parts—Texas, North Africa, and big cities like Washington, D.C.

It was 1958 before I got back to trout streams and commenced turning over rocks in Yellowstone Park streams to find what was under them that would be of interest to a trout. Since I really knew very little about what I was looking for, I did not learn much about the actual nymphs, and only enough about the artificials to realize I was doing something wrong.

The following year found me back in Yellowstone with another complication; the severe earthquake of August 17, 1959, centered twelve miles north of my working base at West Yellowstone, had nearby streams in wild disorder. The continuing aftershocks, some of them fairly severe, put down the fish any time they occurred, and they stayed down for hours.

But it proved a blessing in disguise. A friend invited me to help him secure some whitefish for smoking, and since our local whitefish were just as affected by the tremors as were the trout, we went down on the lower Madison about fifty miles, where the fish were not bothered by the aftershocks. We cleaned and gilled the fish immediately after catching them, and opened their stomachs. I had been examining fish stomachs for years, looking for clues. What I had mostly found was glop. But this time was different, except for a few stonefly nymphs, still alive, the fish were empty; they had just gone on the feed. The nymphs were huge and black and though I knew very little about nymphs in general, I recognized them as *Pteronarcys californica*, and I also knew something about their habits and habitat. I now also knew why the No. 4 Black Wooly Worms we were using had worked.

There is absolutely nothing so intoxicating to the fly-fisherman as to have firm proof that his fly works and also to know what it was that the fish took it for. From that day forward I was and am a firm believer in trying to match the prevalent nymph in a given piece of water and I soon found that the more I succeeded in that, the fewer fishless days I encountered. I still was miles away from being a nymph fisherman but I was firmly convinced that I was on the right road, and the farther I traveled the more I became sure of it.

A couple of years later, only a few years from retirement, I bought some land outside of West Yellowstone, in the Henry's Lake Mountains (but still in Montana) on which to build my retirement home, having decided as early as the late forties that the area contained the best trout fishing in the contiguous forty-eight states, which, of course, it does.

In 1961, I felt I might learn more about nymphs, both real and artificial, if I went down under the water. I had a face mask; I rigged a breathing tube from an old shower hose, hitched up my jeans, and went down for a look.

The first thing I learned was that things look different down there. It was a sort of magic world in which, as a spectator, I could observe the fish, the movements of the natural nymph, and the actions of the artificial when my wife, Grace, drifted them by me. The most surprising thing was that after I got settled into position the fish ignored me entirely as long as I did not make any quick moves.

It was here I learned that updwellings lift line and leader when these lie across them, and that current action turns and twists line and leader, thus causing the fly to turn and roll over and over. Natural nymphs, I found, *do not* roll over and over when cast adrift in the current. Thus, almost always, only the back of a natural nymph would be visible as they drifted along a few inches above the bottom.

This knowledge has led me to tie all my fast-water nymphs "in the round," unflattened and without different back and belly colors. To be dogmatic, which one seldom should be in fly-fishing, they work better when tied that way.

I retired in 1964 at forty-three years of age, moved to Montana, and with Grace's help built our home in the mountains. Since then, except for occasional short periods, I have determinedly worked at learning about nymphs and nymph fishing.

I had long ago decided to restrict myself to coming to know well only a few streams, those close by. I mostly limited my nymph studies to the same streams. However, at first, I did not limit myself to the types of creatures I would investigate

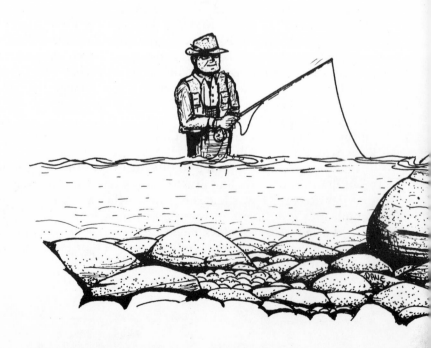

and identify and this was a great mistake. It was 1968 or 1969 before I began to narrow my investigations to the most important nymphs in my streams. I had bitten off too large a chunk.

My education proceeded slowly and by fits and starts. There were many setbacks. But there was an awakening interest in aquatic insects not only by fly-fishermen but also by scientists, and new works began to appear by both that were to be of help. In the course of examining stream bottoms, looking for the standby mayfly nymphs that we mostly heard about years ago, it was forced on my attention that in nearly all streams the caddis types outnumbered the mayfly and in the deep, rocky, very fast sections that the stonefly nymphs not only outnumbered the mayfly but were many times larger. On the theory that, all else being equal, larger trout will prefer the most plentiful or the larger nymphs, I spend more time on caddis and stonefly types than I do on mayfly. In other parts of the country this direction might not be so profitable, but for the area where I live and study I am convinced it is the best way. In the early part of my studies I completely ignored the dragon and damsel fly nymphs. This was a mistake of the first order. Nearly every trout stream contains these predatory insects and their size, numbers, and habits make them among the most valuable to imitate.

As I said in the introduction, the hardest job will always be that of identification. It will also always be necessary; if one does not identify the insects in the streams he fishes, it will do little good to study them.

The student of nymph fishing today will find the road much smoother and easier than the one I traveled. But it will not always be smooth and that's good, because it is human nature to place little value on anything that comes too easily. I think that I can promise you that you will find becoming a nymph fisherman a marvelous challenge.

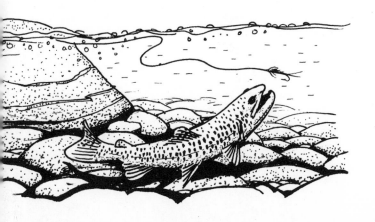

2 The Problem of Identification

EVERY NYMPH IN EVERY TROUT STREAM LIVES IN AN AREA THAT CONTAINS THOSE things it must have in order to survive. This has come about by the process so aptly named by Charles Darwin, "natural selection." Over one hundred million generations, those that selected right, lived; those that did not, died. Thus, the inborn instincts of millions of generations lie behind the habitat selection of the nymph you have just plucked from the oxygen-rich waters that you plan to fish.

How did you come by that nymph? Did it come from under a rock you overturned? Was it netted free-drifting in a slow pool? Perhaps it was clinging to the trailing bine of a waterweed? What! You don't know where it came from? Then what are you doing with it?

You start becoming a nymph fisherman the same way you start building a brick wall. First, you decide where you are going to build the wall, you put down a foundation, and then you obtain enough of the right bricks to do the job. You start with the first brick and you build the wall one brick at a time.

So, you decide where you are going to lay the foundation for becoming a nymph fisherman and you go to that spot on the stream and obtain your first nymph. Then, by catching some more, you make certain there are enough of that kind of nymph in the same piece of water to be worthwhile. An apprentice brick mason must learn to know what kind of bricks will do the job for him, and a beginning nymph fisherman must learn the same thing. You have to work and study to do it.

There must be enough of the same species in each stretch of water for the nymph to be worth imitating; and you will have to identify them in order to know how

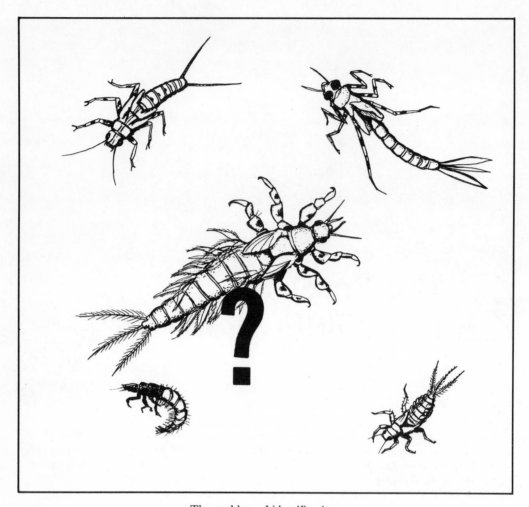

The problem of identification

they live and act, and then to fish a representative artificial in a realistic manner. And you do this one nymph at a time.

In order for nymph gathering to be anything more than a hobby, you must know where each nymph you collect was found, and you must keep some sort of a record of that nymph until you have identified it. As far as I know, there is no other way; if you try to rely on memory, you will soon find yourself hopelessly lost.

I have copped my identifying record method from two different sources: from a rockhound who kept records on each rock and mineral that he found, and from a fishery's biologist who kept such records on fish he studied. I have adapted the best features of both for my purposes.

I use 3 × 5 cards, filled out as the sample below:

FRONT

Card #   Date
Stream
Type Water   Depth
Current Speed   F/Sec. Surface
Bottom Type   Bottom
Description
Weed Types
Prelim. Order
Identity
Exact Location Obtained

BACK

Notes:
Other Types Found Same Time
See Other Card #s

I have emphasized record keeping at the start because I have found that unless your records are easy to keep, and to cross-reference, record keeping tends to get lost in the mechanics of collecting.

Most of my collecting is done with a seine made of common window-screen mesh. I want a nonrusting material and mine is fiberglass, but aluminum is good, too. My seine is three feet by three feet and is fastened to two poles four feet long and one and one-half inches in diameter. About two inches of pole stick out below the bottom; the top portions function as handles. The screen rolls neatly around the poles for storing and hauling.

Around weed beds, individual rocks, and for free-drifting insects I use a standard wire-handled and frame aquarium net, eight by four inches. The mesh is so fine as to be a nuisance but I know of nothing else for close work. You will also need a net for capturing flying forms because they are often required to make identification.

For kill and collecting jars I use simply those small jars in which such foods as pimientos, artichoke hearts, and other such treats come. My wife provides me with them.

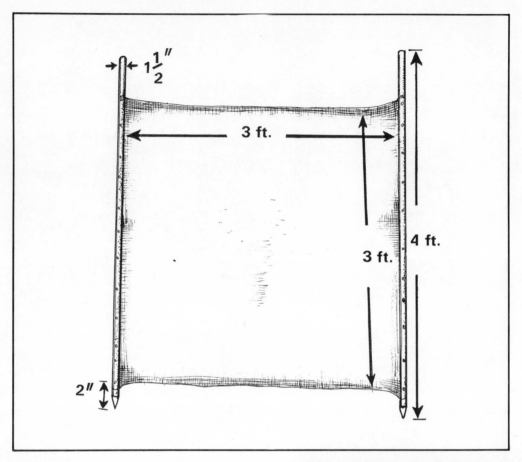

Seining screen

Adding carbon tetrachloride to a kill jar

A temporary preserving solution of 80 percent rubbing alcohol and 20 percent water works well, but if you have to keep the insect a while, it will change color in this solution. Adding a few drops of Formalin to the solution will help delay color changes.

To kill the specimens cleanly and painlessly without maiming them, I put them in a small airtight jar with some cotton in the bottom, covered by a small piece of screen. About ten drops of carbon tetrachloride, dripped on the cotton once every week, will be enough to kill your nymphs, if the jar is kept capped.

Since I use the collecting jars over and over, I do not label them but place the specimen identifying card around the jar and fasten with a rubber band. When I transfer the specimen to a holding jar, I can also transfer the card.

If this all seems like a lot of trouble, let me tell you at once that we have barely begun, and it will never end. There will always be new specimens to collect, identify, study, and imitate. And you *must* keep records.

Basic nymph-collecting apparatus—bottles, labels, tools, and chemicals

This setup is valuable for nymph identification—hole in table, photo floodlight, glass dish

The first two years I spent studying nymphs I kept no records, and as a result, I gained only a little knowledge. I would simply seine the nymphs, put them in bottles, take them home, and start trying to identify them. This sometimes took months and by that time I had forgotten everything else about them. Those first two years were largely wasted.

What do you need to know about the live nymphs in the stretches of stream that you fish? To repeat what I said earlier—because it is important—you need to know their size, shape, and colors to allow you to make a representative artificial, you need to know their habits so that you may fish the artificial in a natural manner, and you need to know their habitat so that you will be fishing the right artificial in the right place. If you do not know all these things, you are fishing by guess, or, as the saying goes, chuck-and-chance.

You obtain some nymphs by seining, from silt, sand, rubble, or gravel bottoms. Push the bottom ends of the poles of your seine into the bottom, holding the screen as taut as you can. Be sure the bottom edge of the screen is on the stream bottom. Then with your hands or a small shovel, you turn over bottom material to a depth of a couple of inches for two or three feet upstream, working with the current to bring any nymphs turned up downstream into the seine. When you feel you have done a thorough job, lift the seine, bottom first, upstream, then lift and carry it to the bank for study.

You may have considerable muck and debris in the seine that will have to be washed out carefully before you can get down to studying what you have. Probably you will have a mixed bag—some mayfly, some caddis, sow bugs and scud, perhaps snails, and maybe even dragon or damsel fly nymphs, although the latter are so active that they usually scamper off the edge of the seine and back into the water while you are wading to the bank.

You are now faced with the first of hundreds of decisions you will have to make in order to become a knowledgeable nymph fisherman: which of the nymphs in your screen are the important ones in the piece of water under consideration? At this point, you are on your own. No one can tell you from a distance which may be the important ones any more than he can tell you how to go to a church social and pick out a wife.

Are there any guidelines for the beginning nymph fisherman? As long ago as 1856, in the fifth edition of his *The Fly-fisher's Entomology*, Alfred Ronalds says: " . . . to an entomological collector the rarity of a species enhances its value; to a fly-fisher on the other hand, the frequent occurrence of a species, and its being widely dispersed or found upon all waters, consitututes the strongest reason for preferring it, because the fish feed upon such species more readily."

(Incidentally, species applied to the taxonomic status of creatures is both singular and plural; the word specie refers to coin or coined money. I make this point because I have just recently read a work on stream insects by a respected author and the term "specie" was used throughout in referring to the final classification of insects.)

→

Gathering nymphs in a rubble-bottomed run. The screen is thrust firmly into the bottom and braced against the thighs.

Ref Card #'s *23, 71*   also, for same insect.
Prelim. order: *Ephemeroptera (Mayfly)*
Identity: *Ephemerella grandis* See card #'s *63, 112, 119*
Exact Location: *3.7 miles above Seven Mile Bridge*
              Notes.

Sample obtained in screen by turning up bottom to depth of 2-3 inches. Several other types found in sample. See Card # a above

Card #*131*   *26 June 73*

Stream: *Madison in Park*
Type Water: *Gliding run*   Depth: *3'- 4½'*
Current speed: *3.5*   f/s. Surface: *Smooth*
Bottom type: *Silt/sand over gravel* general.
Description: *fine material, unevenly deposited in undulations, ridges and hollows. Many weed beds*
Weed types: *Potomegaton natans - P. foliosus most abundant - Ekocharis and Chara also*
Specimen obtained: *by screen seine*
Av. Quantity/sample *3 this type*   No. Samples *3*

Sample record card, front and back.

←

Lean over and rake the bottom material around with the hands or a small shovel. Stir and tumble all rocks and gravel well.

Seining for nymphs

←

Raise the screen upstream bottom first, cupping the center.

Lay the screen out on the bank. There are 17 nymphs and larvae in this catch, of three orders and five genera. But only the large stonefly nymphs (2 genera) are readily seen. You have to examine the debris very carefully to make sure you do not overlook anything.

Turning over rocks while blocking the current from sweeping your find away will sometimes reveal the larger stonefly nymphs. This has to be done quickly but gently. These specimens, taken three days before hatching, are nearly two inches long, exclusive of tails. *(Pteronarcys californica.)*

So, the first guideline in determining the best species in an area for the fisherman to imitate is *frequent occurrence*. That is, there must be enough of that species present for them to be a regular item of diet of the fish. This is the prime reason I *always* take several samplings from different areas in the same stretch of water.

The second and third guidelines I have developed from long observation and study. Insects that are *large* (compared to others in the same area), and those *whose habits expose them to predation by trout* are also important for the nymph fisherman to imitate. Knowing the habits of an insect means it must first be identified so that its habits can be studied. So, there is more than one reason for identifying an insect; you must know why it lives where it lives, and how it acts. The fact that you found it in a certain area is not certain proof that it prefers such areas. It may be that you have found an accident in nature—I have done so several times, and each time it set back my studies. But you will not have this problem very often if you make certain of your identification, then go to the habitat descriptions for that species. The experts who have compiled that information will have weeded out the accidental misplacements for you.

In making that first crucial identification step, you will have had to make some preliminary studies in whatever books are available, so that you may know at once that what you have is either a mayfly, stonefly, dragon or damsel fly nymph—or if it is a larva, a caddis, crane, midge, or something else. Perhaps the best beginner's book on the subject is *Fresh Water Invertebrates of the United States* by Robert W. Pennak. There are several others that may be somewhat easier to digest but none nearly so complete. I would start with this one.

A word of caution: some anglers I know have purchased aquatic insect books that are limited to only one state or a few streams, or in some cases they have bought books on British stream insects, which are virtually worthless in this country.

Before you begin any kind of study of captured insects, you must know the difference between nymphs and larvae, and you must be able to distinguish rather quickly between orders of insects; i.e., order Plecoptera (stoneflies) and order Ephemeroptera (mayflies), plus all others, and this information should be filled in on your identity card in the space headed "Prelim. Order," when you first find your nymph or larva. This is the first brick in your wall.

Once the order has been established we go through the order by family, eliminating those that our specimen quite obviously does not fit. You will probably reach the end of the list of families in that order with several possibles or even probables, which could be the one. Now begins close examination of the nymph with a magnifying glass.

I find that several different powers of lenses are handy: I have glasses of 2.5 to 9 power, and they can be used singly or in combination to give me the resolving power I need. You do not always need the strongest lens to start with. I even bought an inexpensive microscope for studying insects. In my ignorance, which was abject, I purchased one with lenses of 75, 150, and 300 power. All were far too strong and gave too small a field of view. One of 20 power is good, and one of 60 power is about as strong as can be used. But for most purposes, a regular hand magnifier of 5 to 10 power will suffice.

Pennak's book will give you all the information you need to identify your insect down to the order level, unless you have a rarity. But it may not enable you to go further, and go further you must, because it is just about impossible to pin down the activities and habitat of your insect unless you can identify it to the genus level.

Thus, you will progress in your identification through several steps. In the case of mayflies, they will go something like this: order, *Ephemeroptera* (mayflies); family, *Baetidae* (a single group, having similar characteristics); genus, *Ephemerella* (a smaller group very similar in appearance, characteristics, and habits); species, *invaria* (a still smaller group, all identical).

Scientists would argue with the information as I just presented it. It was not written for scientists, or nit-pickers; it was written in order that the serious nymph fisherman would have an understanding of the steps necessary to make an identification of the nymphs in his water.

Perhaps you should know that the streams and lakes of the contiguous forty-eight states contain over 500 species of mayflies, 400 species of stoneflies, 800 species of dragon and damsel flies, 800 species of caddis flies, and thousands of species of crane flies, true flies, scuds, beetles, dobson and fish flies, and other miscellaneous creatures upon which trout feed. It is partly the enormous number of creatures to be identified that has caused nymph fishing to lag. Anglers have been reluctant to commence or are intimidated by the size of the task. Remember, we build this wall one brick at a time, and anyone can do it.

In order to identify your nymph (or larva) to the genus level, it may be necessary to make a step-by-step comparison of the physical characteristics of nearly a hundred pictured and/or described specimens. Finding that many either pictured or described in current books is *the* major problem of identification of aquatic insects. No single book contains more than a tiny fraction of the total number, and if you bought every book ever published on the subject, you would still find less than one-fifth of our trout-stream insects identified by picture or description.

There are some books for the layman that are a big help in that they contain pictures or descriptions of many of the *important* trout-stream insects. The first of these I came across, over twenty-five years ago, was *Professional Fly Tying and Tackle Making*, by G. L. Herter. The descriptions are general, and the drawings in black and white, but this book has enabled me to make some difficult identifications. However, you have to read a basic identification book such as Pennak's before any of the general books mentioned herein will be of much help.

Sid Gordon's *How to Fish from Top to Bottom* has some excellent pictures of various immature forms in it but otherwise is not much help. I could find no help at all in Preston Jennings's *A Book of Trout Flies* or in Ernest Schwiebert's *Matching the Hatch*.

You will find considerable information of great value in *Selective Trout* by Swisher and Richards; while the keys, descriptions, and drawings in this book are mainly aimed at aiding the dry-fly fisherman, there is much incidental information that will be of great help in identifying the more important mayfly nymphs in the streams of the continental United States. It is almost a must book.

A truly must book is *Nymphs* by Ernest Schwiebert. This book contains more information for our purposes than does any other written for the lay angler, and the four times life-size paintings and drawings are an immense help.

Reading Schwiebert's book, one is struck by the staggering amount of work that has gone into it and the voluminous amount of material. One is also struck by what is not there—an identification key and the life histories and habits of many of the listed creatures. The key is not there because there is none that could be of use to the angler, and the life histories are missing because these particular insects have not yet been sufficiently studied for this information to be available. Schwiebert has attempted to bypass the need for an identification key by painting and drawing the creatures so that we may see their form and color. Scientists say that these are not reliable guides to identification; but they fail to say what is, and thus do not provide the fisherman with anything he can use. It is very easy to say what something is not; it is more difficult to provide an acceptable alternative, and in my opinion, Schwiebert has done this better than anyone else to date. His book contains more illustrations of the important trout-stream creatures than any other I know, and it is going to make the serious nymph fisherman's job of identification a lot easier than it has been.

A number of other books contain piecemeal information about various stream creatures, but Swisher and Richards, and Schwiebert, between them have captured the most important of this information.

The largest amount of information is to be found in pamphlets, bulletins, monographs, papers, theses, and other works generally found only in the restricted stacks of a university library. The same is true for ecological and entomological periodicals, which have much special information of value. Use the libraries of your state's universities; they are at your disposal and are gold mines of information.

Thus, we have done our early homework, captured our first nymph, made a preliminary identification down to order, learned that our creature is either a mayfly, stonefly, caddis fly, or something else. Now comes the really difficult part.

There may be other ways, but the process that has worked best for me is to put the nymph in a glass dish in a half inch of water, put the dish over a six- by- six-inch hole cut out of the top of an old card table, then light it from below and above with a couple of No. 1 Photoflood bulbs. Next, I go over it slowly and thoroughly with my hand lenses, trying to pick out the identifying points of claws, gills (number and location), tails, leg spurs, and so on that are given in the various books. Since we do not yet know the family of our nymph, this first step is to identify that. Then we continue, breaking the identity down to genus and finally, if we are able, to species. It may not be possible to go below genus on our own.

When making an identification from order through family, genus, and down to species, do not make a general assumption based on your first casual, streamside glance; if you mistake the order, you will *never* correctly identify your creature.

Four years ago I was seining a long bedrock riffle on the Firehole and my net turned up a nymph that was new to me. That is, I assumed it was a nymph—my first mistake. My next was to place it in the order Ephemeroptera (mayflies). The creature was neither a nymph nor of the mayfly order.

I spent two months trying to identify it and could not find any mayfly family that it would fit into. My state university contacts said it was strange to them. (I later found that they made exactly the wrong assumptions that I had.) Finally I dispatched it to Jim Gilford of Frederick, Maryland, a fellow fly-fisher and amateur entomologist. Before I heard from Jim I happened to be thumbing through Herter's book and a drawing of the creature leaped out at me. It was the *larva* of the riffle beetle, genus *Dytiscus*. In a while I got a letter from Jim confirming the identity.

The larva I had found was immature, less than one-third grown, and there is another very important point: do not make the mistake of assuming that the nymphs are small because they are a small species; it is very possible you have an immature nymph. On the other hand, do not assume the small nymphs *are* immature—just don't let size unduly influence your judgment.

Also, do not depend too much on color at any time. Habitat or bottom type has a distinct effect on color; generally nymphs found in light-colored bottoms will be

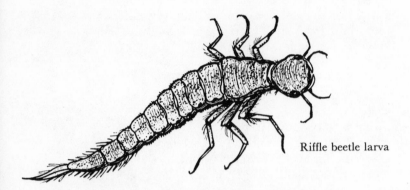

Riffle beetle larva

lighter than the same species found in darker bottoms. However, color *pattern* can be a valuable factor in making a preliminary identification.

You will not collect all your insects by seining. Some, a few, will be free drifting, some will be in weed beds or clinging to rocks. Stoneflies will invariably be found under large stones in very fast water, except for a very few species. But wherever they are found, in most cases habitat will be an important clue to identity.

For purposes of simplicity I use the water and bottom-type nomenclature that limnologists use. There are six important types of each, important from the standpoint of fish and fishermen. The water types, in order of increasing current speed, are pools, flats, riffles, runs, rapids, and cascades. The bottom types, in order of increasing coarseness of material, are sand-silt, sand, gravel, gravel-rubble, rubble, and rubble-boulder. Most insects have a preference for a certain current speed, and bottom-type selection must be right for that insect or it will not survive to become an adult. So it is important to know in what type of water and bottom your insect was found; this will greatly help in identifying it.

You do not have to capture your insects *in* the water in order to obtain the information you are after. If you are on the stream during a hatch, you can capture the adult as it comes off the water, and you may find it easier to establish its identity. You will also know the water and bottom type in which your insect lives and when it will reach underwater maturity—very important information for fishing the nymph. I got this tip from Art Flick when he was out here a couple of years ago and it has been very valuable to me.

Art also pointed out to me that many insects are multibrooded—that is, the same species hatch in groups over a period of days or even weeks; all of them do not hatch at the same time.

This is a survival mechanism. It is highly developed in the *Brachycentrus* and *Rhyacophila* genera of caddis flies, and may account for those insects being so widespread. A multibrooded insect cannot be wiped out completely by some disaster at hatching time, such as extreme cold, high winds, blizzards, or forest fires. I have seen all these happen to a hatch and it is a sobering thing to observe.

Art also told me that he carried his rod with him when he was collecting insects for his *Streamside Guide*, just so other fishermen would not think he was completely crazy. Sometimes, during a big hatch, he said, it was difficult to resist the temptation to stop collecting insects and start collecting fish. He didn't say if will power ever failed him. I think I can guess.

Up to now I have spoken mostly of "nymphs" even when some other form was implied. This is a convenience used by most fishermen, even those well informed on the subject. However, the beginner in the field must be aware that there are other forms of underwater creatures: larvae of caddis flies, midges, crane flies, water beetles, and the like. Then there are the underwater adult forms of scud and other crustaceans that are prime trout food and fruitful to imitate. These may range from tiny water fleas *(Daphnia)* to crayfish in size, and are favorite trout food wherever found.

The caddis are mostly case builders and those that are captured underwater in these cases can usually be identified down to genus by the case. But some do not build cases; they use forms of nets fastened to rocks, and at least one genus, *Rhyacophila*, crawls around on the bottom unprotected. However, most caddis larvae can be identified to the genus level without difficulty.

But the caddis exists in two other forms, pupal and adult, and the pupal form just at hatch time is one of the most explosively effective artificials that exists in the hands of the right angler.

Schwiebert's book will identify *most* of the important caddises in pupal form for you, and will give you the form, size, and color so that you may make an excellent artificial. I like my own pupal patterns better and for those of you who tie flies, these patterns will be found in chapter 18.

Brachycentrus—larva and case

Rhyacophila—larva

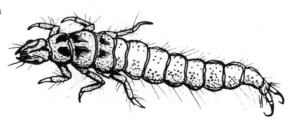

I have used midge, crane fly, and riffle beetle larvae artificials with success, but I have had so little with the crane fly that I no longer bother with it. Midge larvae, in certain weedy ponds, have worked well. I have found specimens to study by digging up the soft bottom and carefully washing out the material in a pan. These larvae differ widely in body color, but the habits of all species are much the same, so one does not need really to identify them. Just find some, so that your imitation may be the right color for the waters you are fishing.

In many waters, crustaceans are quite abundant and form a major part of the trout diet. Here again, identification is not so important, since creatures in this family all have similar habits. Scud *(Gammarus* and *Hyalella)* occupy the same kinds of waters and act much the same. The true freshwater shrimp *(Palaemonetes)* and the fairy shrimp *(Eubranchipus),* while not widely distributed, are similar in habit and habitat and, like the scuds, do not have to be identified below the order level. But you need to know if they are in the waters you fish, and if so, where; and you will need a specimen to imitate.

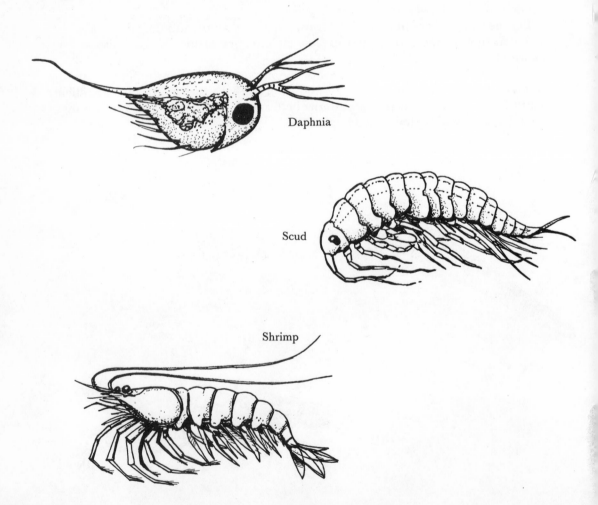

Daphnia

Scud

Shrimp

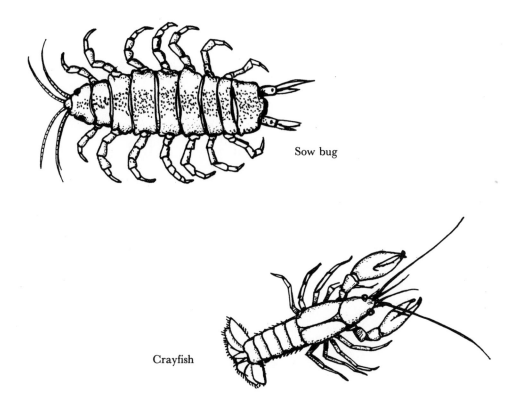

Sow bug

Crayfish

Sow bugs *(Asellus)* need only be identified as being sow bugs, and one specimen is all you need to do this.

The crustaceans are very worthwhile imitating, but are not as easy to fish as most nymphs, since most of them dwell in beds of aquatic weeds and the imitation must be fished just over, or in channels in, the weed beds. But where these creatures are abundant they are a favored food of the trout, and to be really well equipped the nymph fisherman must have the artificial and know how to use it.

The problem of identification will always be a personal task. You will have to find your own specimens, and you will then have to go through most of the identifying process yourself, by going to the books on the subject. And when you fail to make an identification to the genus level, as you often will, you will have to develop your own outside resources to assist you. Whether this is a friend who is a more knowledgeable amateur entomologist, a local professional, or a member of a university staff, it is up to you to develop such sources.

As you can see, nymph fishing is a more personal kind of fly-fishing, because it requires more specific knowledge than any other branch, and the fisherman has to obtain most of the information by his own efforts.

③ Characteristic Nymphs, Larvae, and Crustaceans

ALL UNDERWATER CREATURES, WHATEVER THEY MAY BE CALLED—NYMPHS, LARVAE, OR crustaceans—are tied by certain life requirements to certain current speeds and bottom types. Sometimes one is more important, sometimes the other. Generally, bottom type is more important, yet there will be many cases where the bottom type is suitable for a certain creature, but it will be absent because the current speed is not.

So, one cannot make a blanket assumption that a certain bottom type will *always* hold a certain creature, even if similar bottoms in the same stream do. For that reason, the information presented below will be only generally true. The information is intended for fishing purposes, not identification.

ORDER: Ephemeroptera (mayflies). Generally speaking, this order will be found only in pools, flats, riffles, and runs, with bottom types of sand-silt, sand, gravel, and *finer* gravel-rubble.

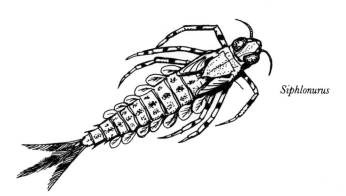

Siphlonurus

27

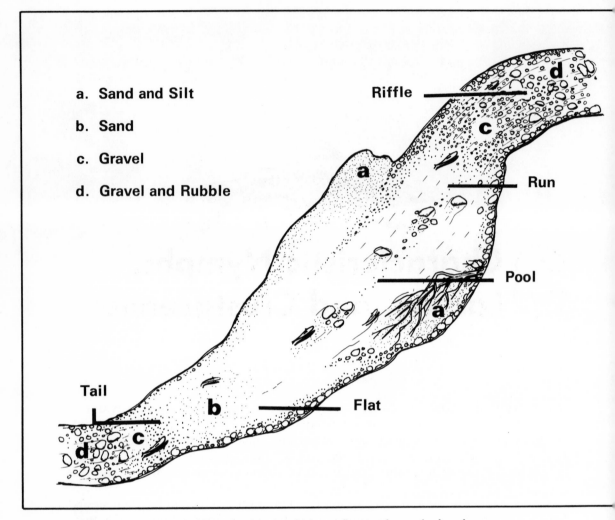

a. **Sand and Silt**

b. **Sand**

c. **Gravel**

d. **Gravel and Rubble**

Sections of a river in which mayfly nymphs can be found

Baetis: These very small mayfiles are important because of their numbers; in many streams they are incredibly abundant. They are very active nymphs, crawling and darting around on the bottom. They are found in more areas of the country and in more streams than perhaps any other mayfly.

The nymph prefers a brisk but not strong current, bottom material of not-too-coarse gravel, and occasionally is found in weeds. It is often found on the current edges of flats and is usually abundant in riffles.

It is multibrooded, hatching throughout the season. It hatches by floating up and riding the surface film. It hatches at times in very cold water and at such times will be struggling in the film for drifts of 30 to 45 feet.

Because of its many activities, the artificial can be fished with a deep dead-drift, deep with twitches, deep with a swimming retrieve; and when hatching, with a dead-drift in the surface film with a curving drag at the end of the drift.

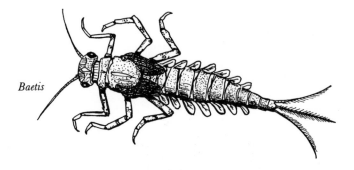

Baetis

Callibaetis: This nymph is found only in quiet waters and smooth bottoms of fine material. It crawls somewhat clumsily and swims with a wriggle. Its hatching manner seems to vary with the species. It is of value mainly because it is multibrooded, and because trout take it readily as it swims from place to place, a few inches above the bottom. Fish with the Live Nymph method, deep.

Ephemera: This, one of the largest of mayfly nymphs, is locally abundant in certain areas. It is a burrowing nymph, preferring quiet waters with fine material no coarser than fine gravel, and will most often be found in pools and flats with a silt or sand-silt bottom. It is capable of swimming fairly well, and some species will be found in waters of fair current speed. They fold their legs back while swimming and are more active on darker days. They come rather swiftly to the surface where they split the shuck and rise quickly from the surface during hatching. Fish with a rapid lifting motion at hatch time.

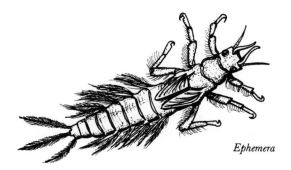

Ephemera

Ephemerella: These are medium-size nymphs of generally dark color, somewhat blocky in shape. They are found in many water and bottom types—pools, flats, riffles, the edges of runs, and in bottoms of silt to fine rubble. They crawl and swim actively, and are a preferred food for trout where found. They swim with their legs folded back and a fishlike wiggle. At hatching time they sometimes split the shuck below the surface. Most of the time they struggle in the surface film for a long time, then ride the surface several feet farther before flying off. These characteristics make it one of the best emergent-type artificials to use just as the hatch is getting under way. Also, this is one of the most widespread mayflies and there are numerous species in the genus.

This nymph's swimming actions are imitated by the Live Nymph method deep, drifting deep with hand retrieve and at hatch time, with a dead-drift in the surface film, with light twitches.

Ephemerella

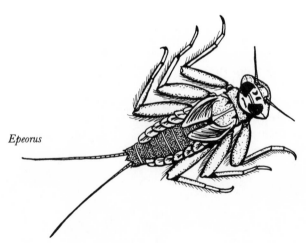

Epeorus

Epeorus: This genus formerly was known as *Iron* and is the genus of the famous Quill Gordon (*Epeorus fraudator*). This genus is distinguished by having only two tails; most mayflies have three.

The nymph prefers moving water and will be found in flats and riffles and on bottoms of gravel and gravel-rubble. It is a clinging, crawling nymph, but when it hatches, it becomes of value to the fisherman.

At this time it usually splits the nymphal shuck a few inches from the bottom and struggles to the surface in a thin membrane, not unlike caddis pupa. An emergent type artificial should be used, using the Leisenring Lift, and a second choice would be a down-wing wet with wings of wood duck, like the Cahill, with the body color matching the emerging natural. My Natant Nylon Nymph is my favorite for this hatch.

Hexagenia: These large nymphs are burrowers, found in slow waters with silty bottoms—pools, flats, and backwaters—and are generally only of value to fishermen when they hatch. They are in the water three years from egg to hatching adult. They swim quickly to the surface to hatch, usually at twilight and on into darkness. This is the time to fish your large artificial with a Rising-to-the-Surface or Leisenring Lift method.

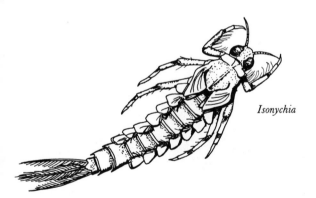

Hexagenia

Isonychia

Isonychia: This is one of the most valuable to the fisherman, if it occurs in his waters. These are medium to large nymphs and they are among the most active of any genus. They swim and dart fearlessly in the bottom layer of even strong currents, and thus are exposed more often to the trout.

The nymph prefers riffles and runs with gravel to rubble bottoms; this same water is much preferred by trout, and thus it is a favored food. They crawl to shallow, still water to hatch and an emergent artificial is of little use. It is not found in very many streams, but where found is most valuable to imitate.

The imitation is best fished with the Live Nymph method, deep, with occasional twitches.

Leptophlebia: This is mostly an eastern and midwestern genus. It is a slow-water, smooth-bottom lover, and sedentary in nature. It is best fished dead-drift along the edge of any current, or hand retrieved very slowly through backwaters and quiet eddies. It is one of the less important nymphs to the fisherman.

Potomanthus: Another genus of slow waters and smooth bottoms. It crawls and swims in the area just above the bottom. At hatching time it moves rather quickly to the surface and the lifting artificial should be given a swimming movement at this time. It is not profitable to use if not hatching.

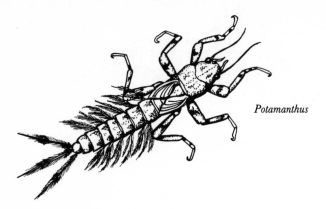

Potamanthus

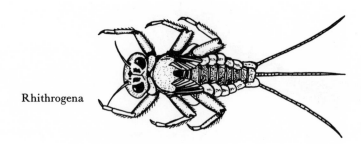

Rhithrogena

Rhithrogena: These are clinging nymphs, of little use to the fisherman through most of the season, but of great value when they hatch. They like good currents and rocky bottoms, but they are seldom off these rocks except at hatching time. They are widespread but abundant only in a few localities. At hatching time they rise rather slowly in the water and the artificial should be fished dead-drift.

Stenonema: Fast to medium-fast water with gravel to rubble bottoms is the preferred habitat of these medium to large nymphs. They are clingers and crawlers, seldom off the rocks of the bottom. The artificial should be an emergent type, fished in the surface film at hatching time. Fish it dead-drift with little twitches. This nymph sometimes takes thirty seconds to shed its nymphal shuck in the surface film, and this gives the fish a good opportunity to feed on them.

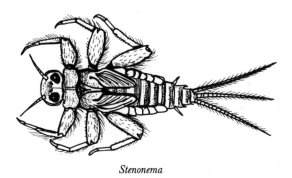

Stenonema

ORDER: Plecoptera (Stoneflies).

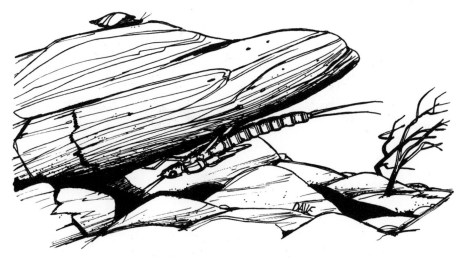

A stonefly holding under a rock

Most of the species in this order need, in fact *must* have, very fast water and bottoms of coarsest gravel to large boulders. Those most important to imitate will be found in fast runs, rapids, and cascades, with gravel-rubble, rubble, and rubble-boulder bottoms. I have found no evidence that any of them can swim.

Pteronarcys: This genus contains the largest nymphs of any in the order. *P. dorsata,* a midwestern to eastern species, is the largest; the nymphs will be about two inches long at hatching time. *P. californica,* the next largest, is less than one-quarter inch smaller. This is a Rocky Mountain–Pacific Coast species and is abundant in the fast, rocky streams of that region. This is the "salmon fly" of the West.

These two are different in habits and in habitat. *Dorsata* prefers streams that have decaying organic material in abundance and will often be found around deadfalls and drifts. They are slow crawlers and do not range widely.

Pteronarcys—side and dorsal views

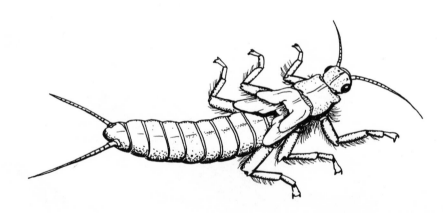

Californica is a rover, one of the widest ranging of all nymphs. It moves not only up and down stream but from middle to shore as it searches for the plant food that makes up 98 percent of its diet. My experience with this nymph indicates that it is not always on the move, but that at least twice during daylight hours this nymph will commence to crawl and clamber about, among, and over the rocks in the stream. When this movement has been under way for a few minutes, with thousands of nymphs crawling over the bottom, trout will commence to feed vigorously on them. These periods usually last from forty-five minutes to an hour and a half.

Acroneuria: These are the next largest nymphs of this order, but the several species in the genus vary greatly in size. Their habits are similar, and their habitat also. As in *Pteronarcys,* they prefer very fast water with gravel-rubble to rubble-boulder bottoms. All are crawlers.

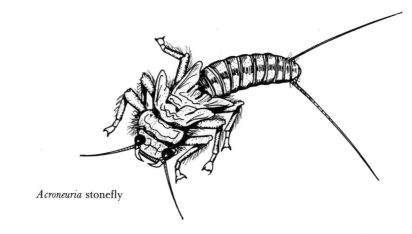

Acroneuria stonefly

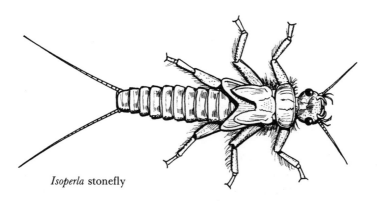

Isoperla stonefly

Perla: These also vary in size, according to species; they range from one-half inch to just over one inch. They like fast water, but will sometimes be found in bottoms of coarse gravel as well as where the bottom material is larger.

There are many other genera, but these are the most important. They are all *similar* in habit and habitat, all are crawlers, and all crawl to the bank or up on rocks, logs, or similar objects in the stream to hatch. All are fished with a fast-sinking or Hi-D line, *on the bottom,* dead-drift. In stretches of streams where they exist, they are the most important nymph for the trout and for the fisherman. They live underwater, from egg to hatching adult, two, three, or four years. Thus, no matter what time of the season it is, the nymphs will *always* be there in desirable sizes and numbers.

There is disagreement among entomologist as to whether *Pteronarcys* has a three- or four-year life cycle. The problem is caused by the fact that the egg of this genus, after being laid, will take from six weeks to eleven months to hatch. There is no known explanation for this delay, which varies by stream and area of the country, but no pattern has been established, and scientists just don't have the answer. In any event, I have never failed to find nymphs in Montana and Yellowstone Park streams of sizes to indicate at least three-year classes were in the stream, no matter what time of the year the samplings were taken. As far as I am concerned, *P. californica* has a four-year life cycle. Also, as far as I am concerned, it is the most important nymph throughout the West. In streams where it lives, I have never failed to take trout with the artificial, and mostly these have been fish of over a pound.

ORDER: Trichoptera (caddis flies).

Taken countrywide, this is probably the most important order to the *fish*. Its members are more widespread, found in more areas, streams, and stretches of stream than any other. There are over 800 species in the order in North America and most of these are stream types.

They are found in every water and bottom type, and where conditions are suitable, they will be unbelievably abundant.

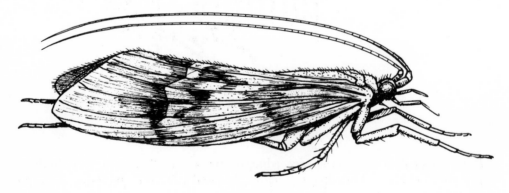

Adult caddis

Brachycentrus: Probably the most widespread in streams; I cannot remember ever seeing a trout stream outside Alaska that did not host this genus. The larva makes a unique case of bark and cellulose matter; it is square in cross section. The larvae range freely over the stream bottom and will be found in most bottom and water types, but prefer medium-slow to medium-fast currents and bottoms of gravel to gravel-rubble.

The larval imitation is fished dead-drift on the bottom. It is only moderately successful, but it will sometimes work when absolutely nothing else will. I will cover fishing the pupal imitation at the end of this section, since the pupal imitations of nearly all genera in this order are fished alike.

Brachycentrus, with case

Rhyacophila: This is the naked caddis; its larvae build no case until time to pupate. The larvae, which roam the stream bed freely, range in color through all shades of green, from light and pale to dark and rich, and some are almost a fluorescent green. They are found in bottoms of silt to gravel, and from relatively still to relatively fast currents. Fish the imitation on the bottom, dead-drift.

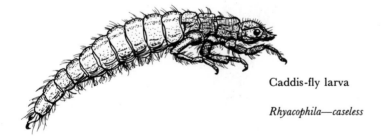

Caddis-fly larva

Rhyacophila—caseless

Hesperophylax: This is one of the larger larva of this order. It makes a case of small rocks and grains of sand, shaped like a fat cigar. It is found mostly in flats and riffles and in the shallow edges of fast runs, over bottoms of sand and gravel. It is not a widely distributed genus, but is sometimes locally abundant. I have found it in rocky California streams in unbelievable numbers. The cased imitation is fished dead-drift along current edges and slowly "crawled" over the bottom where this can be done.

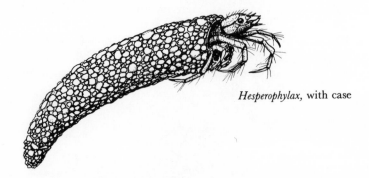

Hesperophylax, with case

Psilotreta: Found around the edges of riffles and other fast currents over sand and gravel bottoms, this larva builds a case of sand grains slightly curving, and tapering, larger at the head. It is much more widespread than the preceding, but the same imitation fished in the same manner will work for both.

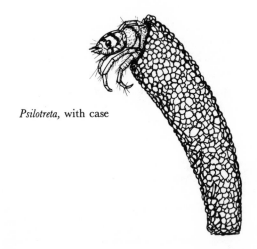

Psilotreta, with case

Stenophylax: A genus of quieter waters and smoother bottoms, also abundant in cold-water ponds and lakes. Its members are large, over an inch long. It builds a case of various materials, mostly arranged longitudinally. I have seen them two inches long in the cold waters of Grebe Lake, their cases made of lily stems and leaf sections, and of sticks and dead stems. They are excellent trout food. A cased imitation of the larva is seldom practical.

There are several other genera that are important to the fish and fisherman. They are not difficult to identify to the genus level by their cases, but are not too profitable to imitate in the cased form. Most of the time it is the pupal form that it will pay us to imitate.

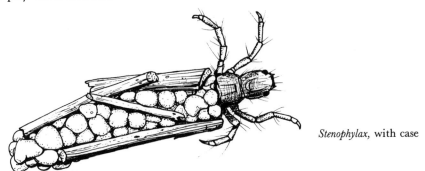

Stenophylax, with case

Many of the caddises are multibrooded, having several periods of hatching during the season. This is especially true of *Brachycentrus* and *Rhyacophila*, and is one of the characteristics that make these two of the very best to imitate.

Nearly all caddises go into a pupal stage, dormant on the bottom, for a few days or weeks. Within the pupal cocoon, anchored to the bottom, they turn into the adult insect.

At hatching time they chew through the pupal cocoon and emerge in the water enveloped in a membranous sac filled with air, with a pair of legs protruding. This air-filled sac causes them to rise rapidly to the surface, and they aid this process with rapid swimming motions of the protruding legs. A few inches below the sur-

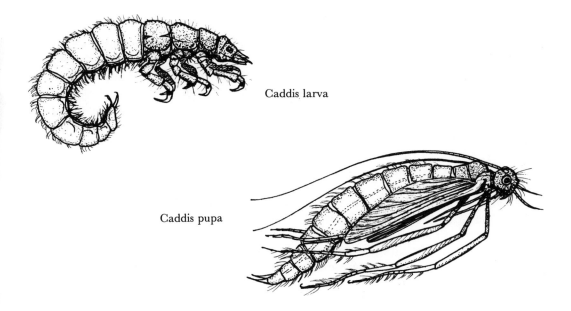

Caddis larva

Caddis pupa

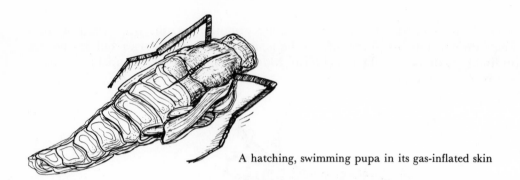

A hatching, swimming pupa in its gas-inflated skin

face, the membranous sac splits and the caddis bursts through the surface like a Polaris missile, flies off, and is gone in an instant.

Their bodies and wings are covered with fine hairs that make them waterproof in much the same way the hairs of seals and otters do; thus, these flies do not spend *any* time on the surface when hatching. At hatching time they are almost worthless to the dry-fly man, but are of utmost value to the nymph fisherman.

Fish them with the Leisenring Lift in spot lies or known holds. When fishing the water, use the Rising-to-the-Surface method. In both methods the fly must be sunk to near the bottom to start with, and for most success, the natural should be coming to the surface to hatch.

ORDER: Odonata (dragon and damsel flies).

Dragonfly nymphs generally are squat and stocky, damselfly nymphs long and tapering. Both are carnivorous, eating other nymphs and larvae, and both swim strongly by taking in water and ejecting it forcefully at the rear. Thus, all members of the order move in little darting pulses when swimming. They cling and crawl well also, and thus may be found in strong currents, but both prefer relatively smooth bottom material because there are fewer places for their prey to hide. Since most are similar in habits and habitat, only one genus of each is covered below.

Libellula: This is one of the largest dragonfly nymphs, some species are over an inch and a half long, as wide and thick a man's thumb. The species range from light tan through darkest brown; some of this variation may be caused by color adaptation to the bottom on which they live. The artificial should be rough and spraggly in construction. It works best fished on a fast-sinking or Hi-D line, on the bottom of pools, flats, riffles, around the edges of runs, and in backwaters. Retrieve in short, sharp twitches of six inches, pausing irregularly. Do not let it dawdle; an artificial this large is readily detected as a fraud if it is retrieved too leisurely.

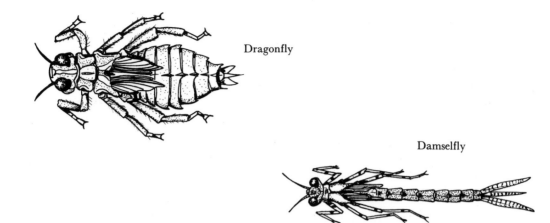

Dragonfly

Damselfly

Argia: This is a rather more robust damselfly nymph than some. It prefers the same water and bottom types as those just listed for the dragon nymph. The species of this genus range through tans and browns in color, all are somewhat mottled, and some have a purplish tinge. Other genera come in varying shades of green. Fish the artificial as described in the preceding paragraph. Both this and the dragonfly nymph imitation are among the very best to use in lakes and ponds. They are both found in almost any water where any other insects are found. Most damsel nymphs can swim slowly by sculling with their oarlike tails (which are actually gills).

ORDER: Neuroptera (fish flies and dobsonflies).

Alderflies are a member of this order also but the nymphs are secretive and not very active and are probably of little use to the fisherman.

Dobsonfly larvae (the true hellgrammite) are among the largest underwater forms found; at maturity they will be three inches long and thick as your little finger. They are found in fast, rocky water, but their range is limited. They are often found in trout streams that hold smallmouth bass. Fish-fly nymphs (larvae actually) are smaller and less widely distributed.

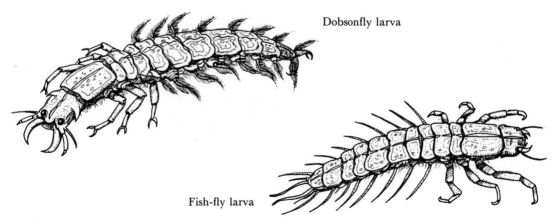

Dobsonfly larva

Fish-fly larva

Corydalis: The nymph is the true and only hellgrammite, though fish-fly larvae and large stonefly nymphs are also called hellgrammites by most fishermen. The hellgrammite is widely used and sold for bait. It is found only in very rocky, fast waters. Since it moves *on the bottom* by hitching itself backward, fish the imitation (which should be weighted) with a Hi-D line; it is best to twitch it swiftly along the bottom.

Chauliodes: This form is about one-half the size of the hellgrammite at maturity and somewhat similar. It is also found at times in slower waters and in backwaters with silty bottoms. It is fished in the same manner as the hellgrammite.

CLASS: Crustacea (prawns, shrimps, and scuds). These creatures are not insects but are of a completely different class of invertebrates in the phylum Arthropoda. In freshwater, they are found almost entirely in weedy waters, where the currents are slow and the bottom material fine. Since the true freshwater shrimp, *Palaemonetes,* is found only in a few waters, it is not covered here.

Gammarus: These are among the larger scuds. They are not as widespread as some other forms. They require alkaline waters and certain weed types and this limits their distribution. However, they are so abundant in some waters as to constitute a major food item of trout. They are most always found in water weeds and the imitation must be fished in the channels and open spaces among the weeds, as deep as possible. Each bed of weeds will pose a different problem and it is hardly possible to detail the methods of fishing them.

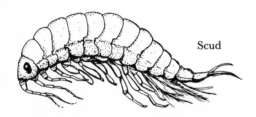

Scud

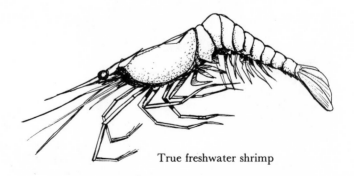

True freshwater shrimp

Fairy shrimp

Hyalella: This smaller scud is probably the most widespread of all scuds; it is found in nearly all trout waters where weed growth is abundant. It is about one-half the size of *Gammarus,* but its actions are the same. It swims and scuttles among the weeds; it is active and usually abundant. It is a favored trout food wherever found. It must be fished as described above, which means you are virtually on your own.

Asellus: Technically, these are in a different suborder than scuds, but no matter. They are found in the same types of waters and weeds, are widespread and abundant, and act much the same as scuds. They are called sow bugs.

All the above listed creatures are active swimmers and scuttlers and any method of fishing them should take this into account. The artificial should be given a lively swimming action at nearly all times.

I have omitted several types and kinds of underwater forms—crane-fly larvae, true-fly larvae, riffle beetle larvae, and other similar creatures. Some of these are found in very few waters, others, because of their habits, are difficult to imitate, others are very limited in distribution. If they are to be of value to the fisherman, it will be on an individual basis, and the fisherman must make the determination for himself.

Of course, this is true of much about nymph fishing. It is up to the individual to find out what creatures are in his waters, which of these are abundant, and what ones are worth imitating, or can be imitated. No form of fly-fishing places such a premium on individual knowledge and effort as nymph fishing; for that reason most of its practitioners are rather solitary and sometimes secretive fishermen.

CHARACTERISTICS CHART OF IMPORTANT NYMPHS, LARVAE, AND CRUSTACEANS

Genus	Water Type	Bottom Type	Moves	Emerges	Fishing Method(s)
STONEFLIES					
Pteronarcys	runs, rapids, cascades	rubble to rubble-boulder	crawls	crawling	*All Stonefly Methods*
Acroneuria	runs, rapids, cascades	rubble to rubble-boulder	crawls	crawling	dead-drift on the bottom
Other types	runs, rapids, cascades	gravel to rubble	crawls	crawling	
MAYFLIES					
Ephemera	pools to riffles	fine gravel or sand-silt	crawls & swims	flys off quickly	dead-drift & Rising-to-the-Surface
Hexagenia	pools & backwaters	sand-silt	crawls	swims up & floats	Leisenring Lift Rising-to-the-Surface
Potomanthus	pools & backwaters	sand-silt	crawls & swims	swims up & floats	dead-drift & Rising-to-the-Surface
Siphlonurus	pools & backwaters	sand-silt	crawls & swims	crawling	dead-drift & hand twist
Baetis	flats to riffles	gravel to rubble-weeds	crawls & swims	pops up & floats	dead-drift & Rising-to-the-Surface
Isonychia	riffles to runs	gravel-rubble	crawls & swims	crawling	dead-drift & hand twist
Epeorus	flats & riffles	gravel to rubble	crawls	pops out flying	dead-drift & Rising-to-the-Surface
Rhithrogena	flats to riffles	gravel to rubble	clings & slides	rises slowly	dead-drift
Stenonema	riffles & runs	rubble	crawls	floats in film	dead-drift & surface film
Ephemerella	flats to runs	sand-silt to gravel-rubble	crawls & swims	pops up & floats	dead-drift & hand twist

CADDIS FLIES

Rhyacophila	pools, flats, & edges	silt to gravel	crawls	pops up & flies off	bottom dead-drift & Leisenring Lift
Brachycentrus	pools, flats, & edges	silt to gravel	crawls	pops up & flies off	bottom dead-drift & Leisenring Lift
Hesperophylax	flats to riffles	sand & gravel	crawls	pops up & flies off	bottom dead-drift & Leisenring Lift
Stenophylax	pools & flats	silt to fine gravel	crawls	swims to edge & crawls out	dead-drift & hand twist deep
Psilotreta	riffles, edges	gravel to gravel-rubble	crawls	pops up & flies off	dead-drift & Leisenring Lift

DRAGON-DAMSEL FLIES

All species	pools, flats, riffles	silt to fine gravel	in spurts	crawls out	On bottom with twitches

ALDERFLIES

Dobson	riffles, runs, rapids	gravel-rubble rubble	hitches backward	crawls out & pupates	hand twist on bottom
Fish fly	pools & backwaters	silt & fine material	crawls	crawls out & pupates	hand twist on bottom

CRUSTACEANS

Hyalella	pools & ponds	weeds—silt	swims	does not emerge	slow hand twist
Gammarus	pools & ponds	weeds	swims	does not emerge	slow hand twist
Palaemonetes	pools & ponds	fine material & weeds	swims	does not emerge	slow hand twist
Fairy shrimp	ponds & backwaters	silt & weeds	swims on back	does not emerge	slow hand twist
Sow bugs (Asellus)	ponds & pools	silt, detritus, & weeds	swims backward	does not emerge	slow hand twist

4 Tackle for Nymph Fishing

ONE OF THE THINGS THAT HAS HELD UP THE ADVANCEMENT OF NYMPH FISHING, WHICH has never been mentioned to my knowledge, is lack of proper lines. We have only had the right kinds of lines for all types of nymph fishing for about six or seven years. Before that, we had floating lines and poorly sinking lines. I don't know of anyone who could be a well-rounded nymph fisherman under that kind of handicap.

We now have full-floating lines, floating-sink-tip lines, floating-sinking lines where the entire shooting head sinks, but the rest floats, and full-sinking lines. Some of these sinking portions will be slow sinking, some fast sinking, some high density (Hi-D), which is fastest sinking of all. And lines are being improved faster than any other item of tackle. So the all-around nymph fisher now has the tackle he needs to do the job.

I own full-floating lines, slow-sinking lines, fast-sinking lines where only the shooting head (30 feet) sinks, Hi-D lines where only the shooting head sinks, and one sink-tip line where only ten feet of the tip sinks, the rest floats. I always have at least four of these with me on extra reel spools in the back pocket of my vest. The one that generally gets left home is the sink tip. I find it less useful than any of the others, but there are situations that call for it and a few where nothing else will work. I wish to emphasize that you *must* have the proper line for the kind of fishing you are doing or you are largely wasting your time.

I know a few nymph fishermen who claim to be serious nymph fishers, who use nothing but a floating line. These people are kidding themselves. The simple fact is that, except at hatching time, nymphs of most species spend most of their lives on or within a few inches of the bottom. There are many more stretches of trout water that cannot be fished with a floating line than there are that can.

We do have a few streams or stretches of stream in the contiguous forty-eight states where nymphs and other underwater forms are found at midwater, but such places are rare. In England, especially in the south, where streams are slow and so full of weeds that they must occasionally be mowed, nymphs will be found at midwater fairly often. This is not England, and while a fish will be taken now and then at midwater in this country, one cannot count on this with any regularity.

So, if you are serious about nymph fishing, get yourself the proper lines.

You can use a floating line when certain types of mayfly are just about to hatch, and when the trout are up near the surface taking most of the insects before they split their shuck. Also, when trout are up over weed beds, just under the surface, floating lines are the ones to use. Fishing nymphs around logs, drifts, and other entangling obstructions in slower water also calls for a floating line, but there are cases when a sink tip will do a better job.

The sink tip is often needed around weed beds where most of the weeds are well below the surface, but where occasional patches reach up to or near the surface and would therefore entangle a sinking line. Many riffles of under three feet deep can be fished with sink-tip lines and they are more pleasant to use than a slow-sinking line. There are quieter waters, much deeper, which call for the sink tip, but generally, unless there are surface obstructions, the slow-sinking line will do a better job here.

My feeling is that in many cases if your line is not entangling or catching on the bottom now and then, you should be using a line that sinks better. In most cases, weed beds excluded, I want the fly to at least *reach* the bottom quickly so that I may then *fish* it up to and at the proper level. It is quite easy to raise the level at which your fly is drifting; it is very difficult to lower that level unless you have exactly the right line.

If you are not pretty much in control of the artificial nymph, you are not really fishing it naturally. Being in control most especially means drifting and fishing the imitation at the proper level with the minimum possible amount of slack. That calls for the proper line, and technique can only be strained so far to replace it.

Even when you are giving the nymph some action, as in the Rising-to-the-Surface and Leisenring Lift methods, you must get the fly down quickly, so that you have time to fish it up *before* it passes your objective or comes straight below.

Therefore, in all nymph-fishing methods, achieving the proper level with the fly quickly is most important. You want to control the line, not have the line control you, which means having the proper line to start with.

Leaders are almost as important as lines in nymph fishing. The tendency almost always is to use too long a leader. This robs the angler of some of the control that the proper line gives him.

In all the surface or near-surface methods, one may use as long a leader as he wishes without sacrificing any control, and often such leaders are an actual asset. But when you want the fly to get to the bottom, it is often not possible to do so if the leader is longer than six feet.

Recently I fished with a man who attempted to fish a pool about four feet deep with a fast-sinking line and a nine-foot leader. The line went down at once, pulling the leader butt with it. But the last five feet of leader and the unweighted fly drifted along two feet above the bottom during the entire drift. It is doubtful if any of the bottom-resting fish in the pool ever saw the fly. All moving water creates updwelling that tend to lift all things in the water toward the surface, especially leaders because they lie across the updwelling.

I prefer very short leaders for most deep nymph fishing, from four to six feet in most cases. Two-thirds of the leader will be a very fast taper, the last third will be a single piece of fine tippet material in most cases. Dry-fly men shudder when they see me making up some of my nymph leaders, because I often knot a tippet of .006 inches to a tapered butt of .011 inches. Of course, such a leader will not turn over gracefully, but if I am fishing the nymph deep or starting it off deep, turnover and delicate delivery are of no concern.

Leader-tippet size for nymph fishing will often bear no relation to hook size, as it often does in dry-fly fishing. What is wanted is all possible flexibility so that the artificial may move as naturally as possible. I will sometimes have a size 6 nymph knotted to a 5X tippet, though this is rare.

In order to avoid trouble when joining up two pieces of monofilament of quite different sizes, I use what is known by most anglers as the nail knot. It was called the needle knot when a bunch of us were using it in the late forties in the San Francisco area, because we used a splicing needle to form the knot. I now use a large darning needle, which is far superior to a nail or tube.

To make the needle knot on a line butt, take the line butt between thumb and forefinger of the left hand, with one and one-half inches protruding to the right, clear of thumb and forefinger. Fold five inches of the leader butt or mono back on itself and grip between the left thumb and forefinger, loop to the left, about an inch from the point of grip. Place the needle on top of line and leader, eye to right, just past the line butt.

Now take the end of the five-inch piece of mono that was folded back and wind it around the three pieces of material *and* the needle, to the right of the left thumb and forefinger. Make four turns only, *to the right,* toward the needle eye. Push the end of the mono through the needle eye, and push the needle to the left, through the left thumb and forefinger grip as far as possible, then grasp the point end of the needle with the right hand and pull needle and the end of the mono through completely. Still maintaining your thumb and forefinger grip, remove the needle, then pull alternately on each end of the mono (leader or whatever) until the knot snugs up fairly snug. Now pull on both ends of the mono at the same time with both hands. As the knot tightens, smooth the wraps with your thumb and fingernails. Keep tightening until all is tight and smooth. Clip off the mono end as short as possible, and the short end of the line butt also. That finishes the knot, but you can coat it with Pliobond or other material to make it smoother.

The illustrations should make it clear how the knot is tied.

Two pieces of monofilament of much different size can be fastened together with this knot, and the knot joint will be smooth and straight and stronger than a blood or barrel knot. I have fastened mono of .006 inches to a piece of .015 inches and had a smooth, strong, straight connection.

The thing to remember in making this knot is that the material to be wound is

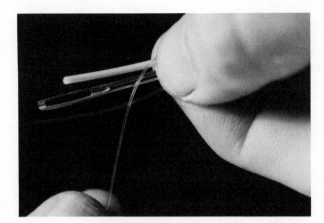

Holding position for Brooks's needle nail knot

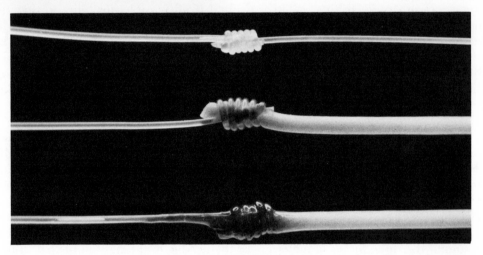

A close-up for Brooks's needle nail knots: *(from top)* leader to leader, leader to line, leader to line (with Pliobond coating).

always folded back on itself, then wound around all material, and the needle, *toward the eye* of the needle.

When you use a needle for this knot, you do not have the problem of trying to push the end of the material through the loose loops or winds that you have made. Just put the end through the needle eye and *pull* it back through those winds. It is much easier.

Large nymphs should be weighted under the body; this will be covered in the chapter on flies. Small nymphs are better unweighted, but weight often must be used on the leader to get the fly down. I use lead fuse wire for both purposes, and for use on the leader, I like a blood knot about a foot from the end to hold the wire from slipping when it is wound tightly and closely around the leader.

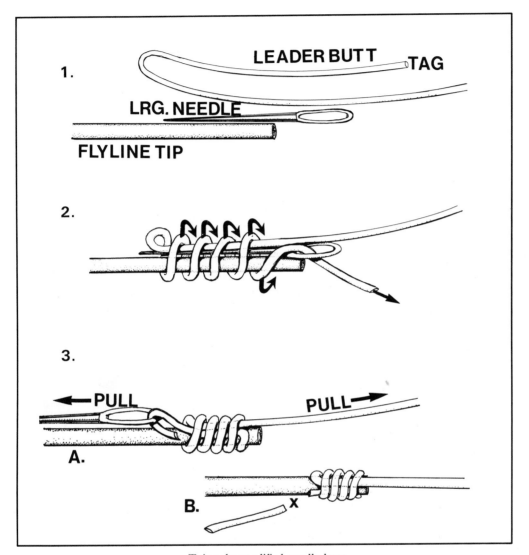

Tying the modified needle knot

How much weight to use on the leader will vary with conditions, but generally I want enough to get the leader point and fly down at once. This is especially true where action is being given the fly. On bottom dead-drift methods, I want enough lead on the leader so that I am getting hung up occasionally.

Unless you tie your own, getting the artificial nymphs you need can be difficult, or even impossible. Nymph patterns have proliferated to an unbelievable degree in the past few years. Most of the patterns available in the shops are formless and nameless, so general in nature they are little better than the hundreds of old wet-fly patterns we have used for years. This lack of names makes nymph selection extremely difficult; there has been no standardization of nymphs or their common names to any extent.

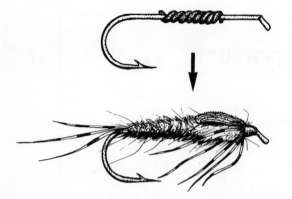

Leading for weighted nymphs

Two ways of leading a line

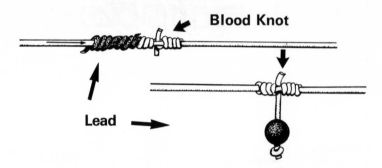

Blood Knot

Lead ➡

For instance, while writing this chapter, I went through my several fly-tying materials and tackle catalogs, and found over fifty nymphs listed in some of them. Most of them were described rather than named (i.e., Graygreen May nymph) and thus are difficult to identify. Some are named for their dry-fly counterparts— Hendrickson, Quill Gordon, and so forth—which is of help, but there are hundreds of live nymphs that do not yet have a dry-fly counterpart. One of the catalogs I have lists over seventy nymph patterns; five were named after the dry fly the natural hatched into, four were named after their creators, some had names of untraceable origin, some had suggestive names, and the rest were more or less descriptive. This is a good example of the thorough muddle we are in with our nymph patterns at present.

How are we going to straighten it out? I wish I knew. Of course, if you collect and identify your own naturals, then tie patterns to imitate them, it is no problem. Or, if you can go into a shop and pick out the ones that suit your purposes, and they are available, again, not too much of a problem. It is when you try to order them from a catalog that you become lost. And some of the best fly shops, making and selling many of the best patterns, are largely mail-order shops.

Perhaps the answer is to have someone with the knowledge and talent of an Ernie Schwiebert make up a catalog of pictured patterns of *all* the most important nymphs, larvae, and crustaceans, with a name for each. This would rather quickly standardize things, but in addition to knowledge and talent, the writer would have to have a rather formidable reputation and enough courage to endure the rage of those whose pet patterns were ignored. Who will bell the cat?

As for now, the only solution for the nonflytier is to assemble his patterns as best he can, then reject those that do not appear to be effective. This is, or can be, an expensive procedure because my experience is that many more patterns will be rejected than will be kept.

Rods for nymph fishing need not be as special as, say, the Frank Sawyer Nymph made by Pezon et Michel. I find that any good rod of suitable length and weight is perfectly satisfactory. I like rods of eight to nine feet, since I find that line control is more easily achieved with rods of this length than it is with shorter rods. With an eight-foot rod, more line can be kept off the water, free of weeds, logs, and rocks; and it is easier to mend the drift than with shorter rods. Line control is the name of the game in nymph fishing. Whatever is needed to achieve it must be done or you might as well take up making doilies so that you will have something to show for your efforts.

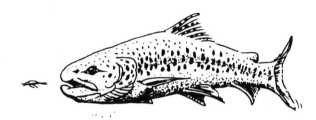

5 Prelude to Nymph Fishing

THE HISTORY OF FLY-FISHING GOES BACK OVER FIVE HUNDRED YEARS IN WRITING AND much farther than that in practice. During that time, like the practice of medicine, it has grown through practice and precept, each generation learning from and building on the knowledge of those who have gone before.

Nothing substantive springs full blown into life, in either theory or practice. It is always preceded by a gestation period that may be only days or perhaps hundreds of years. The latter is the case of nymph fishing.

Although the earliest writings on fly-fishing indicate that the artificial is to be patterned after the natural, the writing is so imprecise (and the language so different) that today we are not sure what fly or what stage of the fly is being described.

The first person to indicate surely that he was writing about the underwater forms was an Englishman, John Tavener, unfortunately, not a fisherman. But in 1600 he published *Certaine Experiments concerning Fish and Fruite,* which contains the first positive mention of immature aquatic insects. Tavener apparently was the first to observe in writing that adult winged flies came from underwater in immature form, to the surface, where they hatched in a short time into the winged adult.

In 1676 Charles Cotton indicates in the first treatise completely about fly-fishing (the fifth edition of Walton's *The Compleat Angler)* that he knew the flies he was imitating spent their immature lives underwater. Cotton's information is confusing, and in error, but he unmistakably knew that his flies were water bred.

Knowledge of underwater life proceeded slowly, and by fits and starts. From what I can infer or deduce from those who wrote after Cotton in 1676 but before

55

Ronalds in 1836, most of them knew their flies were imitations, however crude, of flies that were born underwater. There has been much speculation and even controversy about how those old writers fished their flies, whether upstream or down, whether deep or shallow, whether the often used term "aloft on the water" actually meant on the surface or just in the upper stratum. Also, there have been some later writers who wondered why those early fly-fishers fished a winged adult sunken.

There were at least two reasons for this. One, the heavy iron hooks in use until the mid-nineteenth century made it almost impossible to float any fly, even a well-hackled one. The tiers of those days did not hackle most of their artificials, and those that were hackled were often, nearly always, tied with soft hackle, bird's or capon's feathers. Thus, even if they had intended to fish dry, as the adult form of their imitation would make it seem, hooks and materials would not let them.

But they caught fish, and the forms of their flies, the downwing *adult* wet fly, catches fish to this day. There are still writers who wonder about that. The fact is that nearly all caddises, and at least two species of mayflies, turn into the adult form underwater, and struggle or come up through the depths in that form. Also, many downwing wet flies suggest a mature fly pulling itself free of the nymphal shuck, and there are mayflies that commence this procedure as soon as they leave the bottom. Whether this answers the question of what the fish take them for, I leave to you.

As far as fishing the fly "aloft on the water," this is almost exactly what the emergent nymph fisherman, using the Skues method, does. During the prehatch, a period that for some species of mayflies may last as long as forty-five minutes and during which time the dry fly is useless, the emergent artificial nymph is very, very deadly, and even an old, downwing wet fly of the proper color and size will take many fish.

After Ronalds, in 1836, published his historical *Flyfisher's Entomology,* there was at last a solid foundation for the nymph fisher to build on, even though the book was sketchy on the underwater habits and life history of most of the species described. This would be unusual if it were not so; aquatic entomology as a science was less than forty-five years old when Ronalds wrote his book, although the life of the mayfly was described by Swammerdam in 1738.

Ronalds's work featured mostly the adult insects, which are both easier to catch and to identify, and though dry-fly-fishing as such was little or not known until later, the book was of more value to the dry-fly man. This is unfortunate, for all fly-fishing entomological studies that followed it, except one, were devoted largely or entirely to the dry fly. This includes America's books on the subject, Jennings's *A Book of Trout Flies,* Flick's *Streamside Guide,* and Schwiebert's *Matching the Hatch.* Not until *Nymphs* was anything like a guide to underwater forms available to the angler.

Thus, nymph fishing, when it began to separate from wet-fly-fishing and be called and written about by its own name, had no guide to draw on. There were few nymphs known, pictured, or described when Skues began to think seriously about fishing an imitative underwater form. It is undoubtedly this fact that caused him to fail to make more thorough and direct associations of the artificial and the natural. It is also probable that the lack of such a guide influenced Hewitt in exactly the same way.

Disregarding the nonspecific fumblings of earlier wet-fly-fisherwriters, the history of actual, deliberate fishing the artificial nymph while knowing what it was supposed to represent cannot go earlier than 1900 and probably is closer to 1910.

It is generally considered that Skues in England and Hewitt in the United States were the first deliberate and informed artificial nymph users. Hewitt's work was superficial, and is not of much value to today's nymph fisher. Skues was more thorough but still did not go deeply into the subject. The chief value of both men is historical: they were the first.

However, it may be interesting to show how Skues got started nymph fishing since he was the first and the method he developed is still used.

He, like many others, was taken in by the Halford dry-fly cult in the 1880's, thus when he began using wet flies as a supplement to the dry fly, he did so in a secretive and guilty manner. It wasn't until Sir Edward Grey published his *Fly Fishing,* then the best, and still one of the soundest, books on all-around fly-fishing for trout that Skues began to make his own determination about that course to pursue.

He had, in the course of becoming a devout dry-fly fisherman, noticed that there were many, many hours when no fish were rising, and that many times when they were rising they could not be induced to take the dry fly. The dry-fly man today faces exactly the same situation. Skues's effort to find out what the fish were taking when they were rising vigorously but would not touch a floating fly led directly to the development of deliberate nymph fishing. That was only sixty-eight years ago, and there has been little progress to date that is founded on more than guesswork.

Most of the writers who have written on nymph fishing since Skues and Hewitt have leaned heavily on them or have written in such general terms that they produced little of value.

Let us dispose of nymph fishing and entomological studies done in England; they have little value in this country, and their only worth to us is general. Even Frank Sawyer's *Nymphs and the Trout* has little of *real* value to nymph fishers in this country. He is a mostly one-method nymph fisher and his method has limited use over here.

Ray Bergman was my model as a fly-fisherman and a writer, but the truth is that he cared little for stream entomology and his writings on nymph fishing express only a modified view of wet-fly fishing. John Alden Knight contributed little more; like most writers of his time, his study was severely limited.

Jim Leisenring's little *The Art of Tying the Wet Fly* was good as far as it went, but again, its information is limited in types and waters. However, the method known as the Leisenring Lift is the most effective method of fishing caddis imitations; it also represents the activities of several mayflies at time of hatching.

The work of Ray Ovington, *How to Catch Trout on Wet Flies and Nymphs,* was general, although it contains the first, important *direct* mention of using caddis pupal imitations. The chief objection to the work is that in trying to give it larger appeal, the author glided over the specifics.

Sid Gordon's memorable *How to Fish from Top to Bottom* has some general information on nymphs and a chapter on fishing them. Good as this book is overall, this chapter added little to our store of knowledge that was not previously available. Gordon, although he was greatly interested in nymphs as fish food, did not take the time or trouble to explore their habits and life histories; like most writers up to then, he seemed to think having some good imitations and fishing them in one of several ways was good enough. There is no attempt, except with his wet-dry caddis, to associate live nymph habits directly to methods of fishing them. It is this constant failure to associate the artificial with the habits and motions of the live nymph it supposedly imitates that has caused nymph fishing to move so slowly.

Schwiebert, in *Nymphs,* calls *Fishing the Nymph* by Jim Quick a primer. Its wide scope dilutes the information in it and many of its imitations are worthless or nearly so. Again, in most cases, we have the failure to associate the use of the artificial with the *specific* habits and actions of the natural.

There have been, over the last seventy-five years, a host of articles and book chapters referring to nymph fishing. Many of these have been written by very knowledgeable anglers, but either they were shy on entomological background or they thought their readers were, and have turned out a series of general works that imply that a good nymph imitation fished by just about any method will suddenly increase your catch rate. My experience has been that this is not so, and the hundreds of anglers I have talked to and corresponded with seem to agree with me. I feel that these writings have merely added other types of flies to our arsenal of wet-fly fishing.

This brings us to Schwiebert's contribution. Measured by any standard, *Nymphs* is a giant step toward learning the identity and habits of live nymphs, and it covers more and more kinds of underwater insects and creatures than any other ever written for the angler. There is more information in it of value to today's nymph fisherman than in all works that preceded it. The book's weakness lies in the fact that in writing the portions having to do with actual fishing, Schwiebert tried to combine the literary with the how-to. This is the most difficult form of writing about angling that exists and very few writers have been able to do it successfully. Thus, the methods Schwiebert describes are sometimes obscured by his attempt at a somewhat elegant literary style.

Nevertheless, he is the first to put the horse before the cart; he is quite clear in telling the reader he must know his creature and its habits before the artificial will do him any good. He is probably the most knowledgeable angler we have in both aquatic entomology and fly-fishing for trout, and a fine writer besides: and it is therefore exasperating that he should weaken his masterwork by attempting to make it more palatable.

In rendering judgment on previous works, I have not meant to imply criticism of the authors. It is simply that none of them were full-time writers or fishermen; they had to earn their livelihood elsewhere and in other ways, and they just did not have the time to devote to a thorough study of the matter. Although I am a full-time writer and fisherman, this book will also have its shortcomings. We are light years away from complete knowledge of underwater insects and how to fish their imitations.

In researching for any purpose, it is the contention of experienced researchers that you should obtain five to ten times the amount of information that you can possibly use, because somewhere in that extra material you are going to come upon something very important that you did not recognize when you collected it, because you lacked the background. Therefore, collect everything that you can find on a subject; even if it seems useless at the time.

I agree wholeheartedly with this idea. I was a counterintelligence agent for almost eight years, and the first thing they teach you in that business is to find out everything possible about your subject. It can save your life.

So, after telling you earlier in this chapter to disregard British works on nymph fishing, I must now reverse my field and tell you to read them *if you really wish to become well informed on the theory and practice of nymph fishing.* It is worth reading an entire book just to find one important fact you did not know before. And in order to recognize that it is an important fact, you have to know all the information available on the subject.

Read! Study! Work! There is no other way.

6 The Skues Method

G. E. M. SKUES IS CONSIDERED, BOTH IN THIS COUNTRY AND IN ENGLAND, AS THE FATHER of nymph fishing. Very few anglers seem to know that he started out as a devout dry-fly-fisherman and a disciple of Halford.

In fact, so much a follower of the dry-fly cult engendered by Halford's writings was he that he admitted to feeling guilty the first time he used a wet fly in one of England's South Country chalk streams.

This happened in 1892, and was the result of offering every dry fly he had to a rising fish without results: when he substituted a small dark wet fly and cast it in the same manner, he took the fish. It was exactly a year before he tried the same thing again, under the same circumstances and with the same results. These two incidents started Skues wondering why the wet fly, which had been the only fly used on these streams for centuries, was now considered not only ineffectual but illegitimate.

However, he was too timid to break the recently imposed moral code of the Halford cult that the dry fly was the only sporting method of taking chalk-stream trout, and for seven or eight years he used the wet fly almost surreptitiously to take rising trout that refused the dry fly.

The publication of Grey's *Fly Fishing* in 1899 caused Skues to reevaluate his ideas, and from then on he fished the wet fly deliberately, and with more confidence, and with increasing belief that some of the flies he used were at least fair imitations of nymphs. But his first deliberate and considered use of a nymph pattern came much later, as a result of an accident.

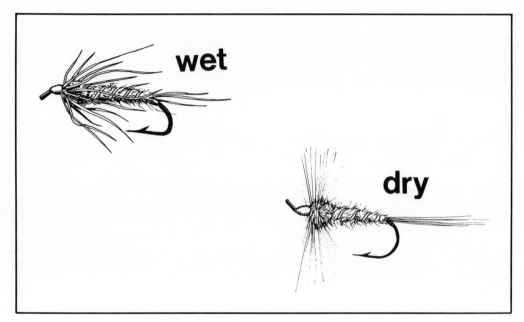

Tup's Indispensable

A friend, R. S. Austin, had originated a new dry fly that he sent to Skues in 1900 to try out on the Itchen. Because of the material used as part of this fly's construction, Skues named it "Tup's Indispensable." The fly was tied with blue-dun or honey-dun tail whisks, a body of primrose (pale yellow) tying silk, a thorax (the first fly made with one) of creamish pink wool, and hackle, two turns of pale blue or honey dun. It may be expedient to note here that British artificial flies, which are mostly very small, often have bodies made of tying silk. They also, invariably, have soft hackle by American standards.

The Skues Method—from underwater, showing the rise forms and the entry of the nymph

Skues had good results with this fly, and used it often. In 1906 or 1907 he was fishing it to rising trout with no success when another of those coincidences happened with which angling history is filled. He was using a commercial fly, made with very soft hackle. In one cast, just in front of a rising trout that had refused it floating, it sank and was immediately taken. Surprise caused Skues to break the fish off on the strike. But he had great success with the fly used sunken, and since he had begun to look at natural nymphs some years before, he noticed that the sunken Tup's had much more of the shape of a nymph than did conventional flies. It was the thorax that made the difference. Skues started using this pattern with hen hackle as a wet fly and found it very good.

It seems that he first tied and used a fly *in direct imitation of a nymph* in July 1908. He is somewhat vague about the dates in his writings, and this is the earliest mention of his tying and using a definite nymph pattern. However, the implication is strong that he was using wet flies in imitation of nymphs several years earlier. If the information above is correct, then it seems the practice of genuine nymph fishing, as opposed to a modified form of wet-fly fishing, began on that day in July 1908.

Those who have only heard of Skues, or who have just skimmed his writings, seem to have the impression that he was totally a nymph fisher and that he scoffed at the dry fly. Nothing could be further from the truth. He was a confirmed dry-fly man all his long life, and repeatedly stated that nymph fishing was but an auxiliary method. This is indicated by the title of his first published work on wet fly and nymphs, *Minor Tactics of the Chalk Stream.*

To understand why he became a nymph fisher at all, it is necessary to have some knowledge of the rivers he mostly fished. These were the Test and the Itchen, England's two premier chalk streams. These are entirely spring fed, and they flow through broad flat valleys over a bed of very porous chalk. In England a stream flowing through a man's land belongs to him and these rivers have belonged to British farmers for over a thousand years. The farmers have tamed and domesticated them to the point that they are much more like canals than trout streams as we know them. The land is pasture and hay land; sod has grown there for centuries and for centuries the farmers have drawn water from these rivers to irrigate their lands. The British call artificially constructed canals "carriers," and the exit from the river into one of these is called a hatch. It has nothing to do with either flies or fish. It is a man-made opening with an adjustable door or gate to control the flow of irrigation water; here in the West we call them head gates. Barriers in the stream to deflect the water into hatches are called weirs and these cause the already slow moving streams to become even slower moving.

There is no such thing as flooding; the rivers can be lowered, but even the most prolonged and heavy rains do not raise them appreciably. This stability is perhaps the most important of factors to the insects, fish, and fishermen.

The second most important thing is their mineral richness. Rainwater, sinking down through sod, creates carbonic acid, which, when it reaches the chalk (calcium carbonate), dissolves it and turns it into soluble calcium bicarbonate, the single most important mineral to plant and insect life.

Chalk streams are incredibly rich in both, and they support an almost unbelievable biomass. The weeds grow so thickly and profusely that they have to be mowed with a sort of underwater mowing machine once or twice a season. Scientists have found as many as 8,000 nymphs per square meter of bottom in chalk streams. British nymph life is mostly small, but it is the mass of it that we need be concerned with to understand both the Skues and Sawyer methods of nymph fishing.

When the eggs of the aquatic flies hatch, the newborn nymph spends a little time in the bottom material. But as he grows, he is literally crowded out, up into the weeds above. As he continues to grow, he overpopulates the weed beds, and weaker individuals are almost continuously forced out, to drift along until they hatch or are taken by fish. The latter is the most common, and results in fish that feed almost entirely on water-bred insects. This is a rich, rich diet, and Skues and other writers have written of sixteen-inch browns that weighed three pounds. In the weed-filled, mineral-rich waters of Yellowstone, a sixteen-inch fish rarely weighs half that much.

Skues thought that all the rising fish he took on nymphs were taking the nymph just before it hatched, but the information on overpopulation was not available to him as it is today. However, from the number of times he mentioned taking rising trout on nymphs for periods of one to two hours without their starting to take surface flies, it seems evident that the fish were taking the nearly mature nymph forced out by overpopulation.

Skues based his belief that the fish he caught were taking preemergent nymphs on his studies of the stomach contents of the fish, which contained all nearly mature nymphs. He also had the mistaken belief that trout did not feed on nymphs below a few inches beneath the surface, based on his stomach studies; no immature nymphs in the fish meant they did not feed on deep nymphs and, therefore, he categorically stated it was of no use to fish the nymph deep. The rapidity of a fish's digestion, and the strength of his own beliefs, prevented him from ever finding out that he was wrong.

One of those beliefs was often stated by him as an injunction; it was wrong at any time *to fish the water in any form.* He would bar any method, wet or dry, that involved casting at random and searching the water. This is so commonly understood on England's chalk streams today as to have the force of common law.

Despite the fact that we do not have many streams in this country (there are some) that have the nymph overpopulations that make the Skues method so valuable in England, it is an extremely useful method during the prehatch, when the water is full of nymphs just under the surface, but few or none have hatched. These periods are generally short. I cannot recall seeing one that lasted more than twenty minutes before the trout switched to taking flies on the surface. However, certain conditions—very cold air, or high humidity, and perhaps others—prolong this activity, and Art Flick mentions that under extreme conditions, prehatch of certain species can last as long as forty-five minutes.

The tackle used, except for the fly, is dry-fly tackle all the way. A long fine leader is a must. Skues regarded 4X as best when conditions allowed its use. I agree, but my leaders for fishing this method would probably give him the shudders. I start off with a nine-foot leader tapered to 3X, then add a five-foot tippet of 4X. That long tippet gives the flexibility needed, and helps avoid spooking the fish.

Since the nymph is usually small, sixteen or eighteen, turnover is no problem unless there is a good wind. If there is, simply fish the fly on the nine-foot 3X leader.

The cast, fishing of the drift, and strike are no different than for the dry fly. You must not line the fish; you cast to the rise, and you strike to the rise. Also, when the prehatch becomes a full hatch, you simply take off the nymph, tie on the proper dry fly, and continue.

Since successful nymph fishing involves fishing the right fly in the right place with the right motion, you already have solved two of the three simply by being there. The trout are taking nymphs just under the surface; therefore, this is the right place. You fish the nymph dead-drift, thus *no* motion is the right motion. All that is left is selection of the fly.

You can find what fly the fish are taking by netting a drifting nymph, or if some have hatched, by catching an adult. I would prefer, however, to have had prior knowledge about what nymphs were in the area. This hatching symptom is con-

→

Glassy surface and weed beds on the surface as well as under it favor the Skues and Sawyer methods here.

fined to only a few mayfly types in this country: *Hexagenia,* which is rarely seen in daylight; *Potomanthus,* not found many places; *Baetis,* the most abundant and widespread; *Stenonema,* excellent to imitate where found; *Ephemerella,* which has one of the longer lasting prehatch periods; and some few others about which little is known, comprise nearly all those that have an extended prehatch period in this country. *Baetis* and *Ephemerella* are by far the most common.

It is good to have some knowledge of when your insect prehatch might occur. Dry-fly men work hard to obtain this kind of knowledge, because it can save hours of sitting by a stretch of water, waiting for a hatch. This is one of the things that drove Skues to the wet fly and eventually to the nymph.

A spot on the Firehole in Biscuit Basin used to have such a dependable hatch in August. It would commence about eleven o'clock and both hatch and prehatch were over by eleven-thirty. Coming upstream (as you should) you passed a little island in the river above which the river curved away to your right. There was a

The Skues Method—casting to a bulging fish

gravel bar at the head of the island, where the stream split. Upstream the water deepened quickly on your left, but remained shallow to the right. In the very elbow of the bend the water near the bank was about four feet deep. The largest fish were here.

When the prehatch activity started, it was always the fish in the shallows just above the gravel bar that started feeding first. These fish were nearly all almost exactly the same size, about twelve inches long. They had to be caught out and released in the fast water below the gravel bar before one could wade up into casting distance of the larger fish. Wading into the shallows where the smaller fish were sent them fleeing upstream and they would put down every fish in the stretch.

Ray Bergman developed a dry fly for this stretch and hatch, which he named Firehole. It had wood-duck wings and tail, cream fur body, and black and grizzly hackle mixed. For the prehatch, a wet Hendrickson of size 16, or the Hendrickson nymph in the same size, was all that one needed to catch all the small fish in the lower end of the run. The same flies would also take the larger fish in the bend, of which there were usually four or five working. They averaged better than two pounds, but I was never able to take more than two on any one occasion, since they fed rather close together, and the disturbance created by the hooked fish put the others down.

It was exactly like dry-fly fishing except for the fly, and Skues's injunction to grease all but the last two feet of the leader had to be followed. If the fly sank more than four inches or so, it was completely ignored.

Sometimes I arrived late and had to fish the dry fly. This took fish as well as the sunken flies did, but I could never catch over three or four before the hatch was over and the rise stopped. The necessity of drying and "blowing up" the fly between each fish took too much time. After several such incidents I became more inclined to nymph fishing the prehatch when conditions were favorable.

The above is a fairly typical prehatch situation. Activity will usually start first in the tail of the pool or run, and in most cases it is necessary to dispose of the fish in the lower section before moving up. However, when overpopulation causes the feeding activity, the situation is different, because feeding will seem to begin in several different areas almost simultaneously. In this situation one must choose an approach that will not spook *any* of the rising fish. On small streams this is usually not a problem, but on large streams it can be and often is.

One of the local streams that sporadically has occurrences of overpopulation of nymphs is the Henry's Fork, especially in the Railroad Ranch section. When this happens, it usually drives the visiting dry-fly-fishermen wild. I have seen these fellows, many of them excellent casters, flog themselves arm weary from fishing the dry fly over nymphing fish. I have seen others move steadily ahead, trying to get past the swarms of small fish rising, to reach the larger fish, only to have the fish quit rising just out of casting range as the angler approached.

This area of the stream is broad, perhaps two hundred to three hundred feet wide, the bottom is uneven, and the weeds plentiful, but often scattered in clumps here and there. There are some very big fish here, rainbows of six pounds and up, but there are droves of small fish, eight to ten inches, surrounding the larger ones, and one must resolutely dispose of these without putting the larger fish down, before any method will avail.

If one has the patience, the right nymph, and uses the Skues method, it can be done. Having the right nymph might be as large a problem as disposing of the small fish; this stretch of the stream contains more species, and even more genera, of insects than any I know. Here one will find *Baetis, Callibaetis, Ephemerella,* and *Tricorythodes* in the mayfly group, some small stonefly nymphs, midge and blackfly larvae, and scud (*Hyalella*). Just finding which of these the fish are feeding on can take half an hour. But until that is done, your chances of success are small.

I have a friend, who when this situation arises, sets out to catch one of the small, less discerning fish. He will do this with some tiny general nymph—Zug Bug, Otter Shrimp, Hare's Ear, in sizes 18 and 20. When he catches his small fish, he immediately kills it and examines the stomach contents. From this examination he determines what is causing the feeding spree, matches it, and commences resolutely working his way to one of the larger fish, which, often as not, he catches. It is a good, empirical solution to the situation.

Thus, the Skues method is, of itself, not difficult, and is effective. In this country the major obstacle to its use is the difficulty of identifying which nymph (or larva) the fish are taking. After that, it is a complete delight.

7 The Hewitt Method

EDWARD R. HEWITT APPARENTLY WAS THE FIRST IN THIS COUNTRY TO DESIGN AND FISH artificial nymphs. Those who have written of Mr. Hewitt have stressed his formal training in chemistry and have lauded his scientific approach to fishing.

Mr. Hewitt may have been scientific in his stocking and feeding of fish, his experiments with light refraction, stream chemistry, and such, but in his writing about nymph fishing, he apparently made no notes and did not even bother to read his earlier writings when he wrote about nymph fishing at a later date.

He was inclined to be dogmatic in his statements, and to change his mind from time to time. Thus, what he said about nymph fishing in his writings of the 1920's will be contradicted by something said in the thirties, and another change will show in his last writings, about 1947. He was fairly consistent in what he wrote of nymph fishing in England, especially in chalk streams, and regarded the Skues method as the one best method. But in writing of nymph fishing in America, he would at different times extol different methods as being the best. However, he was fishing vastly different kinds of streams and what appears to be inconsistency may merely be flexibility—a suiting of the method to the water. This was not clearly reflected in his writings.

There were numbers of errors in his writings, some of them rather careless, such as saying he fished the Madison River in Yellowstone Park about six miles downstream from Old Faithful Inn, and also stating that Billings, Montana, was about 300 miles from Yellowstone Park; the actual distance being a little more than half that. The whole impression I get from his writings is that he cared little about the accuracy of statements he made about things he did not consider important.

The above is not meant as a criticism of Mr. Hewitt, but as a defense against criticism of my designation of his "method." What the reader thinks his method was may well depend on which of Mr. Hewitt's works he reads. However, Hewitt was not only inconsistent in different books; he would give different information in different places in the same book.

In his *A Trout and Salmon Fisherman for Seventy-Five Years,* published in 1948, he in one place states that nymphs in deep water have to be fished at or below the level of the fish, in another place he says they do not have to be fished deep, that the fish will come up for them. At still another point in the same book, he implies he never fishes nymphs in deep water. It is all very confusing.

He apparently knew much about nymph habitat and activities; he repeatedly states that you must fish the right imitation in the right place with the right motion and that success is proportional to the manner in which these requirements are met. This statement may be regarded as the foundation statement of nymph fishing.

I can find little evidence in Mr. Hewitt's writings that he knew or cared about the scientific designation of the nymphs he found and imitated. His writings almost never link a specific natural and its actions to a specific artificial, and for this reason, his instructions are of little practical use, although they may be generally helpful to a beginner.

He made the statement that he considered dry-fly fishing childishly easy compared to nymph fishing and that nymph fishing required far more knowledge, which could only be gained by long study and practice. Also, as a means of catching trout for most of the season, he thought the dry fly much overrated.

He went on to say that he could make anyone a fairly good dry-fly fisherman in a few days, but would not undertake to make a good nymph fisherman in a year, and that it might take several before that person would become a really good performer. Most persons, he concluded, do not do well at nymph fishing because they fish the wrong imitation in the wrong place or with the wrong motion. Here, again, he undeniably knew what he was talking about.

What he calls the best method for nymph fishing was apparently the method he liked best in his declining years. This is fishing the nymph across and down, in riffles, with or without motion. He makes his case for this method on the two assumptions, both basically correct, that more, and more kinds of, nymphs are found in riffles, and that trout prefer nymphs to all other food because of their makeup or food value.

To make the method more than marginally effective, the angler must know what nymphs are in that riffle, and how each of them behaves. Since riffles generally contain several kinds of nymphs, and these look and behave differently from each other, the angler must know what artificial to use, whether to dead-drift it or give it motion; if the latter, what kind of motion. Also, if it is prehatch time, note must be made of the species hatching, and the proper artificial worked in imitation of the activities of that species at hatching time. Seen in this light, there is a lot more to fishing nymphs in riffles than first meets the eye.

Starting with the mayflies, riffles in streams in this country may contain several genera—*Ephemerella, Baetis, Epeorus, Isonychia, Rhithrogena, Stenonema,* and perhaps even others. All of these behave somewhat differently and they certainly do not look alike. All do not mature at the same time so the size of a particular species at the time of fishing must be known. See how complex this is getting, and we have only mentioned *some* of the mayflies. We have not considered caddis, stone, dragon and damsel fly nymphs and larvae, all of which live in riffles. Then there is riffle beetle larvae, which will range, depending on species and time of year, from one-half to three inches long.

The down-and-across method has several variations: just under the surface with dead-drift, with hand retrieve, or with twitches. Or, just off the bottom with the same treatment. The action must not only be suited to the species of nymph you are imitating, but to the particular stage of maturity of that nymph.

Here might be the place to discuss the effect of current speed on the actions of various nymphs and larvae. A number of studies and experiments have been done on this factor, both by groups and individuals. The consensus seems to be that no member of the mayfly group can move against a current stronger than seven-tenths of a foot per second. This is somewhat less than one-half mile per hour. This fact limits the upstream movement of mayfly nymphs almost entirely to backwaters and nearly dead areas except at the bottom. One of those nearly dead areas, the most important one, is just off the bottom.

The type bottom being fished is thus important not only because of the kinds of nymphs it holds but also because of its effect on reducing current speed. Sand or sand-silt bottoms exert only a kind of drag on the current (except in depressions) and this will slow the current only for about one-half inch up from the bottom. This literally limits any movement to crawling. Remember, we are still talking *only* about the mayfly nymphs.

So, if you are fishing a mayfly nymph imitation *on* these type bottoms, it should be crawled over the bottom with a very slow hand retrieve. But few riffles have this type bottom; when a riffle exists over such bottom, it is because the bottom itself is riffled. Such bottoms look like a washboard.

Most riffles have bottoms of gravel. Gravel of pea to large marble size will slow the current down to a livable speed up about two inches from such bottoms. Nymphs, especially *Isonychia* and *Ephemerella,* will swim and cavort in all directions in this two-inch layer of relatively still water. Gravel up to golf ball or somewhat larger size will slow the current to livable speed up as far as four inches above the bottom. So, one must always consider the current speed *and* the type bottom, as well as the kind of nymph being used, before determining how to handle the nymph to create an impression of natural movement. Now it *is* complicated.

Since a mayfly nymph will be the type most often used, let us consider how we might handle one nymph, a fairly mature *Isonychia* imitation, in such a riffle with a coarse gravel bottom. Since this nymph at hatch time emerges crawling, we will not dead-drift it near the surface. But we can use a floating line with a weighted nymph to produce one action this nymph exhibits in riffles.

→

A fast riffle indicates the Hewitt method; depth on the far side calls for a slow-sinking or sink-tip line.

Cast across and down and work the nymph with lifts and dips of the rod tip to cause it to lift up and drop back as it drifts downstream. At times this is killing, at others, if the nymphs are not at the proper stage of maturity, it is ineffectual. If the riffle is more than two feet deep, you might find a sink-tip better than a full-floating line.

If a sunken line is used, it should be for the purpose of imitating the actions of *Isonychia* (we are still talking about this one genus) *on* or *near* the bottom. A line must be used that will allow you to control the action you desire to give the nymph. If you wish to dead-drift it along the bottom, a slow-sinking line might be the right medicine. The line must move slowly enough so that the nymph, in the bottom layer, will not be snatched along at an unrealistic speed. If this happens, you need a faster sinking line or a slower riffle.

The same line that works for the dead-drift can be used (in the same riffle) to give the nymph action: slow or fast hand retrieve, twitches, or an upstream slow crawl. If the line will allow perfect control, the latter method is very deadly. But if the current speed lifts the taut line, then you have to go to a heavy enough line so that this does not happen, because if you are towing your artificial upstream more than a few inches off the bottom, it will fool few fish.

The Hewitt Method—from underwater

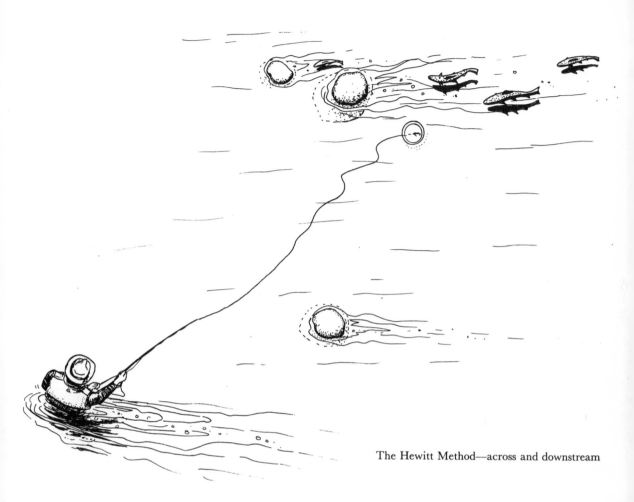

The Hewitt Method—across and downstream

Also, when retrieving your nymph with the upstream crawl, pause frequently. The current action on your long line and leader will cause the nymph to wave back and forth an inch or so each way, and to undulate up and down a bit. These are all very natural movements for this species to make, and sometimes leaving the nymph hang there for thirty seconds or a minute will work where shorter periods do not.

You will probably have to experiment to find which of the above described actions is the taking one for your *Isonychia* imitation *at* the time you are fishing it.

The same methods will work for *Ephemerella* and *Baetis* nymphs but you must slow all actions down, for these nymphs do not move quite so vigorously as *Isonychia*. Also, since these two pop up and float at hatching time, you can fish an unweighted version dead-drift just under the surface during the prehatch. This leaves you in good position when it becomes a full hatch; just remove the nymph and tie on the proper dry fly. The only catch is that you have to be there at just the right time. You will catch more hatches simply by fishing the nymph more. As the fellow said about drinking, it gives you something to do while waiting for your wife to dress, and it is a pleasant pastime, besides.

If you are going to imitate caddis larvae in your riffle, you will, of course, need to know, as always, which ones are there. If I am fishing a larval imitation of a cased caddis, or the naked caddis, *Rhyocophila,* I use a fast-sinking line, a short, fine leader, and crawl the imitation around over the bottom in any direction that I can manage, since these species range slowly but widely over the bottom in all directions.

Dragon and damsel fly nymphs should be fished either crawling on the bottom, or with short, sharp twitches along the bottom. Here again, it is important to know what species inhabit the water. It will not avail to use the large brown or tan *Libellula* when the water contains only the green *Anax* or the small gray *Plathemis*. All act the same but they do not look the same.

All the above are variations of the across-and-down method of fishing riffles. All work, but must be adapted to the time and the species. If this seems a lot to remember, refer to my Characteristics Chart. That is why they are there.

A friend of mine, Gene De Fouw, made up a series of similar charts from information in my earlier books, Xeroxed them, and carries them with him in his fishing vest. This seems a splendid idea. You will still have to know what insects are there, but the charts will help in deciding on the method, whether the Skues or Hewitt in this and the preceding chapter, or perhaps the Sawyer or another in the following chapters.

8 The Sawyer Method

FRANK SAWYER HAS BEEN KEEPER ON THE OFFICERS' ASSOCIATION WATER ON THE WILT-shire Avon since 1927. It is doubtful if any other man has ever become so well acquainted with a stretch of trout water, along with knowledge of all its weeds, insects, and fish, not excepting the great Lunn, from whom Sawyer learned much. Sawyer is also probably the best nymph fisherman England has produced, especially on his own water.

Sawyer spent over twenty years studying the life histories of the insects in his stream, as well as introducing new species, and improving conditions. Like most British fishermen, he does not attach much importance to precise imitation of the nymph; his most used patterns are merely suggestive.

There is a great difference in the makeup of insect structures in streams in England and those in this country. There is only about one-tenth the number of mayfly species in England than there are here; in many British streams there may be only two genera and half a dozen species, and these are mostly apt to be somewhat similar. Also, British streams, at least chalk streams, are so loaded with aquatic life (quantity, not variety) that the fish are little accustomed to feeding on anything else.

→

An almost certain lie for a good fish. The roots on the left mean trouble for any but an almost straight-downstream cast.

79

Sawyer's study of the nymphs in his river produced information that changed the views of entomologists. Before Sawyer's work, it was thought that only a few mayfly species swam; it is now known that nearly all do. Also, when Sawyer first noticed that nymphs moved downstream from weed bed to weed bed, the information was doubted. If nymphs did this, went the thinking, the upstream waters would become depleted, since the nymphs could not move back upstream to replenish the weed beds they had left.

But the nymphs do return upstream, not in midwater, as they came down, but in the near still boundary layer within an inch or two of the bottom. Again, it is believed to be Sawyer who first discovered this.

Thus, the old theory that nymphal forms were mostly passive and inactive has been discarded. Nearly all nymphal forms of the mayfly order are now known to be quite active, those that are carnivorous being very vigorous. Even among those that are not, there are some very active species.

It was also Sawyer who first noticed that the nymphs in his river folded their legs back, streamlined, and swam with an undulating wiggle of the body. Thus, his flies are designed to accentuate this point; the body is the dominant feature. If he uses hackle at all, it is sparse and soft. Most of his patterns are unhackled.

Sawyer also fished the Skues method when the fish were taking just under the surface. These nymphs he hackled so that the hackle stood out from the body, and he did not weight them. Most of his fishing was at midwater, or even along the bottom, and his patterns for this fishing were mostly unhackled and weighted with fine copper wire. This latter fact tells us something about the current speed of the waters he fished. If the speed was much more than one mile per hour, a nymph that lightly weighted would have traveled a long distance before reaching bottom. One mile per hour translates to 1.467 feet per second, very slow current.

This is borne out by the fact that when Sawyer speaks of fishing for trout one or perhaps two feet underwater, he cast ten or more feet upstream in order to have the nymph just at the trout's level when it reached him. This one factor was the major secret of the Sawyer method; the artificial must come to the fish within an inch or two of its level, and either directly in line with it, or not more than an inch or two to the angler's side. It requires great precision in placing the fly and the fish must be visible, since the fly most often is not.

The Sawyer Method—a nymph sinking and drifting to the trout's holding
level

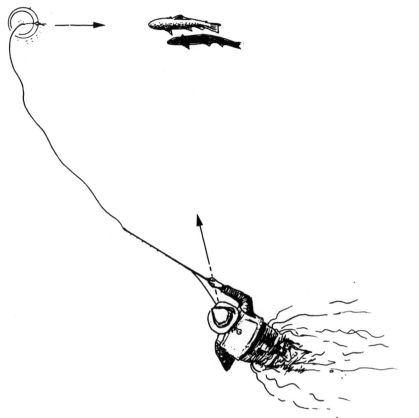

The Sawyer Method—casting up and
across to a visible trout

In this country we have few streams that meet the necessary conditions of very slow current, patches of weed beds with open water between, and plenty of nymphs and fish. There are several that meet some of these conditions but few that meet all.

Here in the Yellowstone area there are some that have very short stretches that are suitable for this method. Current speed is the chief problem. A stream with a current speed of under two miles per hour (about three feet per second) is rare. The problem can be overcome in some cases by weighting the nymph more heavily and by using a sink-tip line. Some fellows prefer, however, to use an unweighted nymph, which they feel acts more naturally, and to get the correct sink rate by using weight on the leader above the fly. These fellows feel that this gives them more control as well, since the weight on the leader can be varied to suit the exact depth and current speed, and obviates the necessity of a sink-tip line. If nymphs smaller than size 14 are being used, the latter method would be better, since very little weight can be added to small nymphs without making them too bulky.

Regardless of how it is handled, the problem must be dealt with in streams. Since one has to see the fish without spooking it on the cast, a slightly up and across cast is most often used. It takes much practice to deliver such a cast precisely yet without extra motion that might send the fish into hiding. Next to locating the fish feeding in such places, this precision of casting, plus the detection of the take, makes Sawyer's method one of the most difficult methods of fishing the fly.

As far as I know, there is no way to become proficient in the Sawyer method except by practice. You do not always need a trout in order to practice this method. In the Bud Lilly Fly Fishing Schools in which I taught for some years, a metal fish on a stand was used. The stand was placed in clear running water about thirty feet out from the student, who then used it as a target or reference point. The purpose was to demonstrate the need for knowledge of current speeds and sink rates. The nymph was brightly colored and the fish was painted bright orange. The students would cast at random at first, since they were beginners, but in half an hour most were able to place the fly so that at least half the time it would move by the fish nearly level with it and just to the angler's side. From my experiences in those classes I believe this to be the best possible method of learning current speed and sink rate effects on artificial flies. And in nearly all methods of nymph fishing, this is of great help.

Even if you cannot see your nymph, and most often you cannot, it is still very important to know the current speed and sink rate. If you know these, you can estimate *about* what level and at what point in the stream your fly is. Even in the Sawyer method you need to know this to determine when the fish has taken your nymph.

The fish may move an inch or so up or down, or right or left, to take a nymph. But if you do not know where *your* nymph is, you have no way of knowing whether the fish was taking the artificial or a natural. If you strike at the wrong time, you will put him down. Many times the fish will take the nymph with no body motion, just an opening and closing of the mouth. You may see this or you may not. But you still must know where your nymph is within narrow limits to know whether to strike. Sometimes the actual take may be detected by leader or line motion, but unless the surface is almost glassy, this motion is so slight as to be unnoticeable. It is better to try to keep track of your fly, by estimating drift and sink rates, at least in most waters.

Since the artificial will be moving quite slowly, a fairly good representation of the natural is required. On all patterns except the very smallest, I like at least one turn of very soft hackle at the head to give a veiling action as well as adding life. Genera to be imitated will include *Baetis,* the smallest and most difficult to use; *Callibaetis,* excellent where it exists; *Ephemerella,* one of the best and most widely distributed; and the smaller species of *Ephemera,* such as *compar* and *simulans.* The scuds and sow bugs, and perhaps midge larvae, are necessary in some waters.

Perhaps the most satisfactory tackle is dry fly all the way. A long fine leader and a fine wire hook are musts. Weight in the nymph or on the leader is required. With a full-floating line, and with the rod low and parallel over the water, the rod should be moved upstream to strike, and the line should be pulled with the left hand. If you come up firmly against the fish, let some line slip through the fingers of the line hand.

This method places a premium on locating the fish, precision in casting, and detection of the strike. Other than that, it is really quite simple.

SAWYER NYMPHS

Pheasant tail

Swimming nymph

Soft hackle nymph

9 The Leisenring Lift

JAMES LEISENRING OF PENNSYLVANIA, BIG JIM FROM ALLENTOWN, AS HE WAS KNOWN, IS
considered by all the many fine fly-fishermen who knew him to have been the most
skilled wet-fly fisherman in the East, and perhaps anywhere. His little *The Art of
Tying the Wet Fly* appeared in 1941 and was lost to view soon because of the war. It
has since been reissued, but for two generations or so it was in limbo.

Nearly all knowledgeable fishermen who read the book know that it was much
closer to tying and fishing the nymph than it was to tying and fishing the tradi-
tional wet fly. Leisenring's flies were chosen for color and action more than shape,
because in most cases, he was fishing it during the period of its life in the stream
prior to hatching and he felt that action was more important than shape. He
obtained the action not only by the motion he gave the fly, but by using soft hackle
that would enhance such motion and make the fly appear alive.

He was insistent on the color of his wet flies being an exact match of the *back*
color of the nymph he was imitating and that the nymph matched be from the very
waters in which the artificial was to be fished. He never says so, but the implication
in this form of tying is that the fish do not see the belly of a nymph unless it is at the
surface during prehatch. At least that is the way I read it, with benefit of hindsight.
Since I did underwater studies of artificial flies some ten or twelve years ago, I have
also given up artificials with different belly colors. I have found them not as effective in moving waters as one tied with only a color matching the back of the
natural. Also, in moving waters, I have come to using hackle all around the fly, and
not jutting from the sides, or bearded underneath. I arrived at this conclusion only

after noticing that any sunken fly attached to a line and leader is turned and rolled by the action of moving water on the line and leader. This rolling over and over, showing back, belly, and all sides, is completely foreign to *live* nymphs; *they do not turn upside down while alive.* Thus, the fish does not see the belly of the real nymph unless he is looking upward at it.

There is a lot more in Leisenring's little book than meets the eye. Also implicit in it is the fact that Leisenring matched the actions of his artificial to the actions of the live nymph during its normal underwater period. Yet, all that most anglers know about either Leisenring or his manner of fishing is based on the Leisenring Lift, a method that imitates the action of the nymph only at hatching time.

There are several reasons why this method became so well known: it *appears* to be an easy method, it works at times and places where no hatch is taking place, and it will even work using an artificial that does not rise to the surface to hatch. Thus, the method has a lot in its favor, and appeals to many fishermen because it *seems* to be uncomplicated, yet often successful.

Leisenring Lift—raising rod to swim flymph
to surface

Leisenring used it only for individual fish, either fish that he could see, or ones whose exact lie he knew. For him, it was a very precise method, and as he used it, it is probably the most deadly nymph method known.

Fishing to a visible fish, or to the lie, the method was the same. Leisenring would study the location, the currents, the precise lie of the fish, the wind, and any other factors that might affect his cast, and then decide what was the best position to be in to make the cast. He would already know what nymphs were in that piece of water and have chosen his fly accordingly.

The fly had to be cast far enough upstream so that it would be on or below the level of the fish when it reached a spot some two feet upstream of the fish. Also, the fly had to be dropped at such a spot that the current would bring it downstream in exact line with the fish. Thus, Leisenring had to be familiar with both the current speed and the sink rate of his fly.

When the fly reached the chosen spot, some two feet upstream of the fish, on or below its level, and in line with it, Leisenring would bring the line taut, and the rod

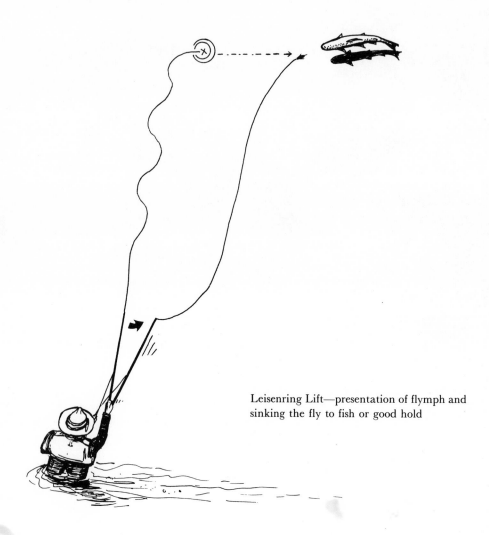

Leisenring Lift—presentation of flymph and
sinking the fly to fish or good hold

tip would be lifted from a point low over the water to full overhead in a smooth
even lift. This is where the method gets its name.

It is almost 100 percent effective used in this manner, unless the angler spooks the
fish by his own actions. And it is one method where a good imitation is not required. The action of many mayflies and nearly all caddis species, several hundred
of them, at hatching time is well imitated by this method. So well do the fish
recognize this that the action is apparently irresistible to them. The method will
actually work with imitations, the natural of which are never seen in the area being
fished. It seems here that action alone is the most decisive factor.

I have experimented considerably with this method, trying to determine if the imitation used is of much importance and I have come to believe that it is not. One example, among many, may suffice to show this.

I was fishing a smooth glassy glide of considerable depth when I came upon a sizable trout in a pocket lie where he could be seen easily and approached within ten feet. Apparently the depth, over four feet, gave the fish a feeling of security, for he appeared confidently at ease.

The bottom was sand-silt, with weed beds. I knew from studies and long experience that the insects in the stretch were small to tiny. I also knew no stonefly nymphs existed upstream of this lie for over a mile.

I tied on a huge black stonefly nymph, No. 4, 3XL. It was very heavily weighted for fishing very fast rocky runs. I dropped the nymph about eight feet upstream of the fish. It sank like a stone in the quiet water. I coaxed it downstream with the rod tip and a tight line, along the bottom. When it was about two feet upstream of the fish, and well within his view, I brought the rod to the overhead position with an even upward lift. The nymph came off the bottom in a smooth rising arc toward the surface.

It never reached the surface. The trout, which had paid no attention to the nymph tumbling gently along the bottom toward him, nailed it savagely as it lifted past his nose. He was nearly twenty inches long, no gullible yearling. Yet, he had taken an artificial that was nothing like, and many times larger than, the naturals that inhabited the area. I have had similar things happen many times while using the Leisenring Lift, and I regard it as the deadliest of all nymph techniques, properly used, for taking larger trout.

As I have indicated, choice of fly is not critical. Yet, I have more confidence in this or any method if my artificial has at least some resemblance to the natural. For this reason, my first choice usually is a caddis pupal imitation, in most cases, Little Grey or Little Green Caddis described in the pattern section.

Though I seldom fail to take a visible fish when using the Leisenring Lift, there are times when it doesn't work. When it doesn't, it appears as though I have somehow alerted the fish and made it wary. When this happens, the trout doesn't flee to seek security; instead, it settles down to the very bottom, and lies there motionless and in plain sight. It is then impossible to raise the fish with anything short of a stick of dynamite. In the past few years, when I was teaching fly-fishermen nymph methods, the most difficult point to get across was that such fish could not be taken.

I remember one such student in particular. He had fished over several fish in the twenty-inch class with this method, and had put them down in the manner just described. But he persisted in continuing to work the fish with other methods, in spite of my telling him nothing would work. In the course of trying everything—dry, wet, streamer, and several nymph methods—he spent more than two hours. I considered the time wasted. But my student did not. If he had learned nothing else the whole day, he said, he would consider it a day well spent. It would save him countless hours of wasted time in the future.

I confine my use of the Leisenring Lift to visible fish or to known specific lies. Used in this manner, it is the surest underwater method to take large trout of any I know.

In the mayfly family, *Ephemera, Hexagenia, Potomanthus, Callibaetis, Epeorus, Rhithrogena, Stenonema,* and *Ephemerella* all come to the surface at hatch time in a downstream rising arc, perfectly imitated by the Leisenring Lift. Because they rise quickly, but have a long drift in the surface film, I prefer the Skues method for *Baetis, Rhithrogena, Stenonema,* and *Ephemerella.*

Nearly all caddis species come to the surface in a quick downstream rising arc, and since we have more caddis species in more of our streams, I believe their presence is responsible for the deadly effectiveness of the Leisenring Lift. I also believe that the apparent conditioned response to this action by the fish is responsible for the many strikes one gets at the end of the drift with other methods. The rising arc at this time, caused by current pull on the line and leader, may be considered as a stream-caused Leisenring Lift.

Typical flymphs

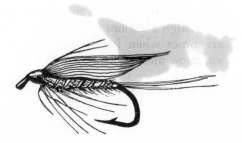

10 The Rising-to-the-Surface Method

THIS METHOD HAS BEEN DESCRIBED BY SOME AS A REPEATED SERIES OF LEISENRING LIFTS used to fish the water. That is a fair description, and while it does not require the preciseness of presentation of the lift in order to be more than marginally effective, the artificial must be a fair to good imitation of a natural found in the stretch being fished.

In fishing either method, the line used must be one that takes the fly down *very* quickly. If the bottom is relatively free from obstructions, I prefer a very fast-sinking, or even Hi-D line. I want the fly on the bottom as quickly as I can get it there, so that I can control how and where the lifting action will occur.

If there are bottom obstructions, one may have to use a sink-tip line with a very fast-sinking tip. Also, leaders should not be over seven and a half feet, about 3X. In both methods I usually want some weight on the leader a foot or so ahead of the fly. This weight actually appears to enhance the action of the Rising-to-the-Surface method.

The cast usually is across or across and down. It is not often possible to control the fly in this method when it is cast upstream and is drifting toward you. After the cast, when the fly has had time to sink to the bottom, take in the slack, then lift the rod tip from low over the water up to the eleven o'clock position smoothly and evenly. Immediately drop the rod tip back to about two feet above the water; at the same time recover the slack. The slack must be taken in swiftly so that strikes, which often come at this time, will not be missed. Yet, this must be done carefully, so as not to move the fly. This is important, and requires some practice. Then the sequence is repeated over and over until the leader comes to the rod tip, even if, at that time, the fly is being worked straight upcurrent. I have had many hits with this method when the leader was just about to enter the tiptop.

The method is a favorite of many anglers, especially those who like to give the fly some action constantly. It is a very effective method of covering the water, and the action given the fly enhances the chance of its being seen by a fish.

It can be an effective method anytime, but it works better if some sort of insect activity is taking place. This often depends on water temperature, and in streams in this area this method works best when the temperature is between 58 and 64 degrees Fahrenheit.

It will be productive during almost any prehatch period of may and caddis flies, and during the prehatch of *Siphlonurus* and *Leptophlebia* of the mayfly group, it is *the* most effective method.

These two, when preparing to hatch, grasp something on the bottom, and take in air to help buoy them to the surface. But they almost never take in enough the first time. Thus, when they release the bottom, they rise a little way, while drifting downstream a little way. Then they drop back, grasp the bottom, and take on some more air. They release, head for the surface, which they may or may not reach. If not, they continue to repeat the process, bobbing up and down, a little higher in the water with each lift, until they reach the surface and fly away, or are eaten by a trout.

Caddises take air into their pupal shuck while still in the cocoon on the bottom. When they chew through the cocoon, they rise swiftly to the surface, burst through the surface, and are gone. Thus, it would seem the up and down movement of this method is not a good one to imitate the action of the caddis at this time. But it works, probably because of the many naturals in different stages of transition— some wiggling free of the cocoon at the bottom, some at every level between bottom and the surface, all of them in motion. After this activity is well under way, it is probable that the trout's greed reflexes cause it to hit anything in motion that has the right color and size. The trout instinctively knows that this glut of feed will soon be gone and must be gathered *now*.

There is a stretch of the Yellowstone in the Park, between the Sulphur Cauldron upstream to Le Hardy Rapids, that has unbelievable hatches of *Brachycentrus* caddis in late July and early August. At this time, using the Rising-to-the-Surface method and a good imitation, or even a dark-bodied No. 12 wet fly with partridge hackle, the number of fish one can take and release (this is a no-kill area) can reach fifty or more. A strike can be expected on every second or third lift, and nearly every fish will be hooked.

If one is on the stream before this activity commences, the stream will appear barren. Hardly a fish, or at most, a few tiny fish, will be in evidence. But as the sun warms the very cold water, one can begin to see fish moving out of the depths, sliding into shallower and shallower water over the clean gravel. As the fish move, with an insinuating wriggle, they are taking caddis commencing to work in the cocoon in the gravel.

The first fish will be the smaller ones, eight to twelve inches. As activity progresses, more and more fish will move onto the gravel shallows, until the bottom has a working fish on every few square yards. It is not unusual to be able to count forty

Deeply sunken weeds and potholes in the bottom provide current relief for large trout in this gliding run. The Skues, Sawyer, Hewitt, Rising-to-the-Surface, and Leisenring Lift methods are all successful at different times, and mayfly, caddis, dragon-damsel fly, midge, and blackfly all are here.

or fifty fish within view once the hatch is well under way. After about ten to fifteen minutes, the fish will be working higher and higher in the water, as the numbers of insects reach an almost saturation level. At this point there will be many sixteen- to eighteen-inch fish in sight, and one can concentrate on working the fly to these larger fish.

One day in August 1974, I took three students to this stretch to teach them the method. The place chosen was a wide curving run, about a foot deep on our side, four or five feet deep toward the far bank. The bottom was coarse gravel with potholes.

When we arrived only a few tiddlers were in sight. But as we were rigging up, a few somewhat larger fish began to sidle out of the depths. At this point we were joined by two students I had been teaching other methods the day before, and the wife of one of these.

As the men began wading into position, activity rapidly increased. In vain I exhorted them to cast short and lift smoothly to maintain line control. After fifteen minutes, during which I grew hoarse and the action frantic, I retired to the bank and joined the wife to watch the spectacle.

The river was now full of feeding fish, hundreds of them, twisting and turning, slashing at the rising caddises. The men were casting furiously, sloppily, switching directions in midcast, ripping the line off the water to slap it down somewhere else. The air was filled with moans and groans of anguish, and cries of exasperation, as they missed fish after fish.

The woman and I chuckled at the exhibition, for it was hilarious. The anglers were catching some fish, but were missing or losing a dozen for every one caught.

The uproar lasted about an hour and then was suddenly over. The men waded ashore, limp from exhaustion. When I gave the most experienced of them a reproving glance, he raised his hands in surrender.

"All right," he said, "I know if we'd listened to you we'd have caught ten times as many fish. But none of us were prepared for anything like this. And even though I goofed right and left, it's been the happiest occasion of my entire fishing life and one I'll remember for the rest of it."

I might mention also that all the men were so sore-armed the next day that they had to forego fishing. But they all sturdily insisted that it was worth it, and they had learned a lot, even if most of what they had learned was what not to do.

This method is workable in almost any water type other than rapids and cascades. Pools, flats, riffles, and runs all surrender fish to this method. As mentioned earlier, it works better if a fair imitation of a natural in the area being fished is used. Like the Leisenring Lift, it will sometimes bring fish to strike an artificial nymph that in life never displays such action.

In the fall of 1972, I was fishing Hole Number Two on the Madison in Yellowstone Park when I was joined by three men whom I had met along this stretch many times over the years. For this reason, although the run is less than two hundred yards long, we all fished it at once.

This could be done without interfering with each other only if everyone knew the drill. We took up station in the stream about seventy feet apart, one above the other. I was in position number two, counting from the tail up. John Rose was in last position upstream. We were all fishing fast-sinking lines and big, black, weighted stonefly nymphs, dead-drift along the bottom.

After each fifteen or twenty casts and drifts, each of us would move, in unison, about ten feet downstream, and repeat the performance. As each man reached the end of the fishworthy water, he waded out and reentered at the top.

As I was walking up to reenter the head of the stretch for the second time, I noticed that John Rose had switched from the dead-drift to a modified form of the Rising-to-the-Surface method. Since we were all experienced at fishing this stretch, and the four of us had been fishing it for a half hour without a strike, I figured John was getting bored with the inactivity.

While I watched, he hooked a heavy fish, worked it into the shallows near where I was standing, landed and released it. It was a brown of about three and a half pounds. Within five minutes John had repeated the performance with an almost identical fish.

We all commenced using the method, but none of us got another strike. When we gathered round at the end of the session to compare notes—always a valuable step—we agreed that John had, by accident, lifted his fly on two occasions just as it was approaching the hold of the two trout. In effect, his Rising-to-the-Surface method had been more of a blind Leisenring Lift. Its success came from having matched the three criteria of nymph fishing. He had used the right fly in the right place with the right motion, and was successful in this case even if the motion was foreign to the fly being imitated. It appeared that, in some cases, the wrong motion could be the right motion if it was one that the fish was conditioned to recognize as natural to many underwater insects.

Whatever the reason, the lifting actions of this method will often produce strikes when all else fails. But learn to keep the line under control or you may never know you have had a strike.

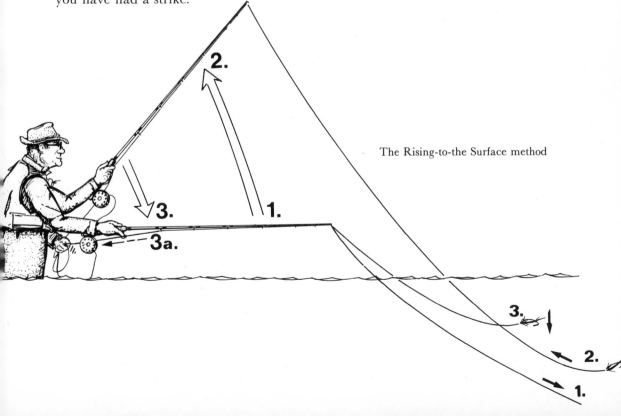

The Rising-to-the Surface method

11 The Upstream Method

THIS IS A METHOD OF LIMITED APPLICATION. SINCE CURRENT SPEED, MORE THAN ANY other factor, limits its use, let's talk more about that subject.

Ichthyologists say that a trout can spend extended periods in currents of no faster than .8 foot per second, but as the current speed increases the energy expenditure increases far more rapidly than the current speed and this cuts down quickly on the amount of time a trout can spend in such areas. If a trout cannot find an area of slower current speed, he will simply die from exhaustion. This is what happens to most hatchery catchable trout dumped in large numbers into a small area of a stream. A trout *must* have some form of barrier to slow the current to a livable speed.

Therefore, when you see a trout in a moving current, his manner will tell you about the current speed at the spot where the fish is holding. If he is barely moving fin and tail, he is in a relatively dead spot. If he appears to be swimming easily but steadily while remaining in the same place, the current will be moving about four feet per second. If he is swimming hard without gaining, he will be in a current of about nine feet per second. Almost any trout you see moving with a steady swimming motion, without changing his location, is either there to feed *or* he has been driven from his lie by some threat.

Current speeds in a stream vary considerably between bank and middle, between top and bottom, and in spot locations. All these differences are caused by friction of some sort. The bank causes drag, so the current in most cases will be slower next the bank than farther out. The atmosphere causes drag, so the surface will be slower than just under the surface. Bottoms exert drag—the rougher the bottom, the more

Note the fins and tail of each trout. (A) is a trout in slow water; (B) is the same trout in faster current; (C) is the same trout in still faster current. swimming very hard

drag. Water moving at six miles per hour (about 8.8 feet per second) over very rough rubble bottoms will have a boundary layer of slow water at the bottom that may be six inches deep. That is why trout can survive in such waters.

Logs, rocks, hummocks, and depressions all slow water down. Weeds, especially in dense beds, exert tremendous friction, and will cut current speed sharply.

Below is a chart of current speeds in miles per hour and feet per second (rounded off to the nearest hundredth).

CURRENT SPEEDS			
FPS	MPH	FPS	MPH
1	.68	11	7.48
2	1.36	12	8.16
3	2.04	13	8.84
4	2.72	14	9.52
5	3.4	15	10.2
6	4.08	16	10.88
7	4.76	17	11.56
8	5.44	18	12.24
9	6.12	19	12.92
10	6.8	20	13.6

One way to make a rough check of the current speed at the surface is to lay out a measured stretch along the bank, say fifty feet, then toss a block of wood onto the surface at the upper point and time it while moving with it to the lower point. If it takes ten seconds to travel this distance, the current speed is five feet per second, or 3.4 miles per hour. That is a pretty stiff current.

I find that most anglers tend to misjudge current speeds badly. I fish the deeply sunken stonefly nymph in a series of very fast rocky runs hereabouts. Since they are the most reliable bets to produce fish of a pound up, on a day-to-day basis, I often take other anglers along. Some of them look at the churning currents and declare a fish cannot live in such water.

I ask these fellows how fast they think the waters are moving. Most of them guess between fifteen and thirty miles per hour. Actually, at high water, in spring, the speed is about eight miles per hour and at low water in the fall, it is about six miles per hour. A speed of thirty miles per hour translates to forty-four feet per second. A straight upstream cast of forty-four feet with a floating line would have the fly straight below in two seconds, an obviously ridiculous situation.

I find that I cannot handle an upstream cast and drift with adequate line control if the surface current is faster than three feet per second. That speed means a one-yard strip with the line hand every second. Any faster than that is pretty frantic action for a supposedly contemplative recreation. And, as I have said, if you do not have good line control, you will not have consistent results.

Mostly, the upstream method is used in quieter waters. If fish can be seen, one casts to them in a way that will bring the drifting nymph to them in a natural manner. For most fishing in the upstream method, the tackle is dry fly excepting the fly itself. Also, mostly it is a somewhat blind casting method, fishing the water, rather than to a known lie or a seen fish.

The most difficult thing about it is detecting the take. Thus, while no more skill is required in the casting and handling the drift than in the Skues and Sawyer methods, it is far more difficult to use with success than either of these. It is possible to have several hits on one drift and never feel or see any of them.

The first time I became fully aware how difficult this method could be, I was fishing a small, crystal clear stream in Maryland in the late forties. I had fished a small gray nymph upstream in the dry-fly manner for about three hours, during which I had a half-dozen hits and landed two small fish. At least, I thought I had only those few hits.

I had just fished up through a narrow gliding section with high banks, when I became aware of a grizzled old man in overalls sitting on a rock at the upper end of the glide. When he saw that I had noticed him, he spoke.

"Been fishing the nymph long, son?" he inquired kindly.

"Just a couple years," I replied.

"Thought so," he said. "You had at least ten hits comin' up from where I first saw you. You never struck once."

"What do you think I should do?" I inquired.

"Well, if it was me, I'd fish from the bank 'stead of wadin'. That way, you'd see most of the takes. These banks are high enough to blot out your figger."

I took the old fellow's advice. I was casting short, twenty-five to thirty feet,

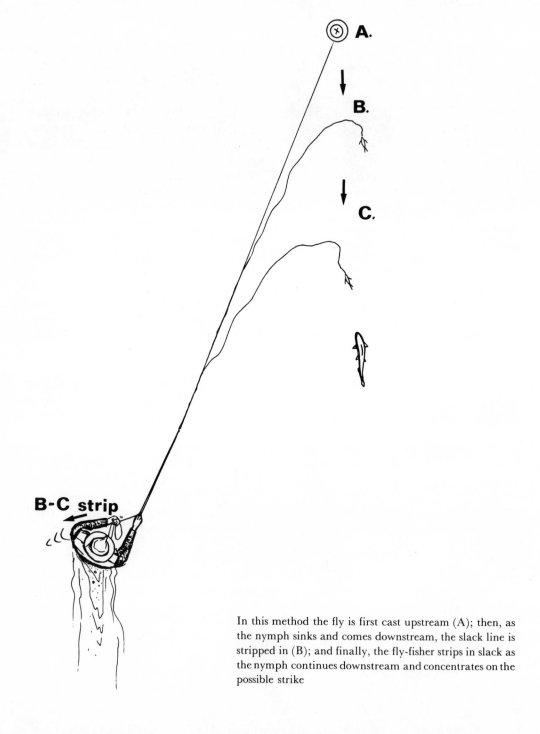

A.

B.

C.

B-C strip

In this method the fly is first cast upstream (A); then, as the nymph sinks and comes downstream, the slack line is stripped in (B); and finally, the fly-fisher strips in slack as the nymph continues downstream and concentrates on the possible strike stalking carefully, and I found I could see not only the fish but even my nymph, which was never more than a few inches deep.

All the fish took in about the same manner. They would move slightly over to intercept the slowly drifting nymph, and softly suck it in. Sometimes they would pull it in from as much as four inches away. Yet, though I could see every take clearly, I could not hook those fish.

After missing at least thirty, some by striking before the nymph was in the fish's mouth, some after the fish had spit it out, I was in a high state of frustration. I stopped fishing and sat down to think things over. While doing so, I remembered something Ray Bergman had written about exactly such a situation. Ray had decided not to strike, but just to study and watch to see if he could detect anything other than seeing the fish take that might offer a clue to striking.

I did just that, fishing and observing everything about the take, but making no attempt to hook the fish. It was educational and changed my thinking considerably.

On most of the takes, even when the nymph was sucked in from three or four inches away, there was no way that the take could have been detected other than by actually seeing it. At no time did the line slow, pause, or speed up. At no time did more than the last foot of leader move perceptibly. There was no above-surface indication of any kind. Even the old trick of a fluffy dry fly at the leader-line connection would not have helped.

What did help was greasing the leader down to within a foot of the fly. Then and then only could I detect any on-the-surface movement. The floating leader caused fewer takes, but by striking to the indication of leader movement at the point where it sank, I began to have a much higher percentage of success, though I still failed to hook more than one of three.

The upstream method is not, of course, a directly upstream method; such casting would put line and leader over the fish and result in few takes. One actually casts a little right or left of straight upcurrent, and fishes a dry-flylike no-drag drift. In blind casting, one covers the water as thoroughly as possible, using all best judgment as to where the fish might be. It is an exhausting method because of the intense concentration required to detect the strike, and in most cases, greasing the leader down to within eighteen inches or a foot of the fly is a great help.

I prefer spot casting most times, especially on larger streams, delivering the fly to pockets in the bank or in weed beds, alongside of logs or drifts, at the front or alongside of rocks, or any place that just looks fishy. I sometimes start off with the dry fly, fishing it in precisely this manner, and if no rises are forthcoming, I switch to the nymph.

What nymph? Well, what nymphs—and larvae—are in the area? Mostly, I find the smaller mayfly species and midge larvae most successful. The best—if they live in the water being fished—are *Stenonema*, *Ephemerella*, and *Baetis* in the mayfly group. I use my Cream Wiggler larvae imitation, and sometimes a small (16 to 18) Hare's Ear, when I don't know what else to use.

Fishing the method with the sunken line, in the channels between weed beds or under sunken logs and rocks, is far more difficult than when the floating line is used. One angler of my acquaintance finds it so difficult that he describes it as "trying to push a car uphill with a rope."

I no longer even try to fish the upstream sunken line except in channels in the weeds. The other places are just too tiring and frustrating and success is not great. But in the weeds, it is often the only method when the fish are deep.

Here one is faced with the problem of "lining" the fish, although the fish themselves are seldom directly in the channels. But even when they are under the weeds they are close to the channel and are bound to see the line as it sinks.

What to do? There is no complete answer in this or any manner of nymph fishing. Sometimes I use the Bergman method of letting the nymph and line sink to the bottom and lie there for two or three minutes before slowly retrieving with a patient hand twist. At other times it works better to start retrieving as the fly sinks. It is largely a matter of trial and error. Generally, the trout are not frightened by the sunken or sinking line if they do not see or feel it hit the water.

Frankly, my advice is not to use any of the upstream methods unless you are in the mood for deep and complete concentration. If you are not, the method will be frustrating. But if you are, the very difficulty of the method can make success in its use most satisfying and enjoyable.

And that's what fly-fishing is all about.

12 The Continuous Drift

THIS METHOD, WHICH HAS TWO VARIATIONS, IS NOT WIDELY KNOWN OR USED, YET under certain specific conditions, it is very effective. And it is one of the easier methods.

The method was first shown me by Larry Phillips of El Portal, California, in 1946, when we were both living in that village on the banks of the Merced River. That is, Larry showed me his variation. I picked up the second on a small meadow stream from watching another angler, and from Ray Bergman's *Trout*. More about the second variation later.

Larry's method was suited to fishing the long shallow riffles that make up the river just below El Portal and on toward Bryceburg. The method is simple; one casts his nymph on a long line across and down and then wades quietly downstream at as near the same speed as the fly is drifting as one can manage. The whole effort is expended in trying to maintain a drag-free drift as long as possible. The drift can be continued even after the fly comes straight below for as long as the water is suitable and *if* the line is long—forty to sixty feet, fisher to fly.

Also, one can pick up, recast, and start a new drift at any time, although Larry believed (and he was enormously successful with the method) that one should leave the fly in the water until something forced one to pick up and recast, or a fish took.

The required condition is a series of long riffles, one after the other, that are relatively shallow and not faster than three miles per hour. Attempting to wade any faster than this is strenuous, and over gravel-rubble bottoms such as the Merced had in this section, it could be dangerous. A nasty fall is quite possible if the water is too fast or the bottom too rough.

A floating line, long leader, and weighted fly work best. The fly should be representative of the largest of the indigenous naturals. Around El Portal a No. 8, 3XL black stonefly nymph was the best bet. But such riffles are prolific in the variety of nymphs, and many different artificials do well. A black, brown, or olive green Wooly Worm in 6 or 8, 3XL, works fine most places.

This is a good method for those who like activity and who like to keep moving. It allows one to cover a lot of water and the fly can be steered into the best spots as one moves along.

I often use this variation from the bank, although there are few places where this is possible. One such is the long riffles connecting Hole Number Two, Hole Number Three, and others on the Madison in Yellowstone Park. This stretch runs through rather meadowlike areas; there are paths along the bank that one can use when pursuing this variation, for these are fishermen's paths, never far from the water. They pass among scenes of great beauty, which the fisherman never sees, for if he is a fullhearted fisherman, his eyes know no greater beauty than the stream itself.

All is not completely idyllic, however, because of the beavers in this section. These otherwise industrious and admirable animals dig tunnels from the river back into the meadows. At a distance of five to eight feet from the river's edge, they drill an escape shaft to the surface. It is these that cause the problem. In more than twenty-five years of fishing this area, I have fallen into these traps countless times. Last year was no exception, but the results were serious. A few days earlier, I had injured my back when a ladder slipped. On this day in August, fishing with Bob Holmes, I fell into one of these holes for the umpteenth time. However, I was unable to loosen up and take the shock because of my injured back, and I hurt myself badly enough so that I wound up in the hospital.

So, when fishing this method be careful!

The second variation, called "bank walking," is limited almost entirely to meadow streams, where banks are even and the water deep right at the bank edge. The type line used is immaterial as only the leader dangles from the rod tip in this method. The leader should be short, six to seven and one-half feet, about 1X. The fly should be chosen to represent the largest natural nymph known to be in that stretch of stream.

With the rod and arm extended full length, and the fly as nearly as possible on the bottom, the fisherman proceeds downstream at current speed, trying to see that the fly is neither dragged along nor impeded. When the fish hit, a return strike is not necessary. I have had fish hit so hard while using this method that they have jerked the rod tip into the water.

Almost any nymph pattern representative of a natural known to inhabit the stretch being fished will work. The fly is being fished downstream in a continuous dead-drift, which just about all underwater insect forms do at one time or another during their life-span.

There must be deep water near the bank or deeply undercut banks. The angler must move steadily and quietly, not jarring the bank with his steps. He must also stay back from the water as far as arm and rod length allow. When done thus, it is a surprisingly successful method for larger trout.

Ray Bergman called the method just described "floating the bank," and first saw it used in California, which is where I also first saw it used.

The wading method is called "roving" by the British, who most often use it with a live minnow rather than an artificial nymph.

The bank walking variation of the Continuous Drift method is excellent for deep water near undercut banks. Beware of beaver holes!

A long, long, shallow riffle; perfect for the wading variation of the Continuous Drift. Your fish are apt to run small in such shallow riffles.

13 The Live Nymph Method

THIS IS PROBABLY THE OLDEST METHOD OF FISHING THE ARTIFICIAL NYMPH IN THIS country; it springs from a very old method of fishing the wet fly, and from attempts by early nymph fishers to give a natural, swimming motion to their fly.

It can be, and has been, used in pools, flats, riffles, and slow-to medium-fast runs. By varying the speed and action of the retrieve, it can simulate the activities of nearly all the mayfly group, a few of the caddis, most stoneflies, all the dragon-damsel fly nymphs, and other underwater forms. It can be used over bottoms of sand-silt, sand, gravel, and gravel-rubble. Thus, it is used in more water types, over more kinds of bottom, to represent more kinds of creatures than any other method.

The above would make it appear that this is the most universally used and effective method of fishing the nymph. The first assumption is probably correct, but the second, regarding its effectiveness, depends on how well one follows the three dicta of nymph fishing—using the *right artificial* in the *right place* with the *right motion*.

Thus, if I am fishing this method (and I do), I want to use a nymph that I know lives in the stretch and I want to use it with the right motion.

Most of the mayflies use two forms of locomotion during their underwater life. They crawl and they swim. To simulate crawling, one needs a line, leader, and nymph that will act together to keep the fly on the bottom. If the current is moving more than two feet per second, this is going to require some weight on the leader. I know a fellow who fishes nymphs on the bottom in very fast riffles and runs; in addition to a fast-sinking line, he puts as many as six large shot on the leader, about a foot apart. When this rig sinks to the bottom, which it does almost instantly, it just lies there, until the angler commences his retrieve. With this setup, the nymph can be moved with a slow hand twist, a fast hand twist, a start-and-stop motion, with a stripping action, slow or fast, and with a twitch-and-hop. All are effective in proportion to how well the motions resemble the actions of the natural that the fly is supposed to represent.

Do I recommend the above way of fishing the nymph on the bottom? Well, if catching is a large part of fishing to you, yes. It will catch fish. But if fishing for fun is your bag, no, I don't recommend it. It is an awkward way of delivering a fly, with none of the grace and rhythm of normal casting. The line has to be swung and tossed like a lasso, and this is an uncomfortable and tiring way of doing what should be easy and pleasant.

Since we have our fly on the bottom already, let's see what actions are used with what artificial.

Damsel and dragon fly nymphs can be crawled over the bottom with a slow hand retrieve, or they can be retrieved with short twitches. Scuds, if in the area, can have a rapid scuttling motion with frequent stops—a fast hand retrieve with pauses.

Ephemera, Hexagenia, Potomanthus, Siphlonurus, Baetis, Isonychia, Stenonema, Ephemerella, and some other less important nymphs of the mayfly group all crawl slowly and their actions can be imitated with slow hand retrieve. Since *Rhithrogena* and *Epeorus* are more clingers than crawlers, it is not usually profitable to use these two imitations on the bottom. All *cased* caddises crawl slowly along the bottom; thus, the very slow hand retrieve is the only method to imitate these types while they are in their cases. All stonefly imitations can be slowly hand retrieved on the bottom *if* the current is slow enough to permit this. Most stonefly nymphs are definite fast-water dwellers.

In all the above actions, the fly is cast across and down; line, leader, and fly must go to the bottom at once, and the hand retrieve commenced at once.

Some of the creatures mentioned above also swim. It is this action that most persons try to imitate with the live nymph method. It is a more pleasant way to fish than the on-the-bottom variation.

One must keep in mind that no member of the mayfly family can move upstream if the current speed is more than one mile per hour. Therefore, it is generally not productive to swim a nymph upcurrent, unless the fly is kept close to the bottom, or unless there are backcurrents where the fly is being moved.

For the most part, most aquatic insects that choose to swim do so just above the bottom *or* they move in a down or down and across manner.

It is this last that works best most of the time. The cast is down and across or directly across, and some form of retrieve started at once.

If the current is two or three feet per second, you will have more success if you do not force the fish to come up too far from his lie in order to take the nymph. Keep the fly down, by whatever means necessary—sinking line, weight on the leader, or whatever is needed.

In the mayfly group, *Ephemera* is one of the slower moving or swimming nymphs; therefore, a slow hand-twist retrieve is used—about ten completed hand movements per minute. *Potomanthus, Siphlonurus,* and *Ephemerella* swim a bit faster, and the retrieve should be made with about twenty completed hand movements per minute.

Baetis swims more rapidly yet, about thirty twists per minute would be the right speed for these small nymphs.

Isonychia is the most active of the mayfly nymphs; it swims fast (relatively) and with erratic darting movements. Sid Gordon called them "bucking broncos." This nymph's actions may be imitated with the fastest possible hand twist, with stops and starts, twitches of the rod tip and little stripping motions, all interspersed to give an uneven, erratic, darting motion. They are favored food wherever they exist, because their actions expose them to the trout more often than do their somewhat sedentary relatives.

All damsel and dragon fly nymphs swim in short pulses, with pauses. The artificial should be retrieved with short, sharp strips, with pauses every third or fourth strip, and the speed of the strips and the length of the pauses should be varied.

Scuds, shrimps, and sow bugs are more often found at midwater than are other forms, especially around weed beds. Most of them swim erratically, with little darts and pauses, dead-drifting during the pause. They also move up and down, so that lifting and dipping the rod tip a few inches each way gives a good lifelike motion.

The basic moves of this method, then, are the across, or across and down cast followed by some form of action to cause the fly to move. The movements are varied to suit the actions of the natural the fly is meant to represent. With fly and line on the bottom, the actions of the creature while crawling are imitated. When the line, floating, slow-sinking, or whatever, drifts with the current, the actions of the creature while swimming should be imitated. It is the many different creatures, with their different manner of locomotion, that makes this method complex.

Simulating one action of one creature is quite simple. Just keep your creatures separate in your mind and the rest is easy.

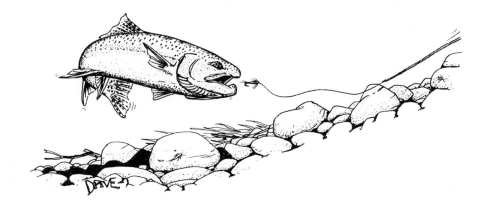

This bouncing riffle can be fished equally well with the Hewitt and Live Nymph methods.

14 The Pot-Shooting Method

WHILE THIS IS A METHOD OF LIMITED APPLICATION, IT IS SO SUCCESSFUL WHERE CONDI-tions favor its use that it has to be included. Also, in the areas where I have used it (the West and northern California), it is the best blind method for taking larger trout.

Some fellows, who use both large nymphs and huge dry flies, call the method "pocket picking." In either case, the method is the same, but the tackle and fly are different.

The water type is pockets of quiet water in very fast water—rapids or cascades. The quiet spots are caused by barriers to the current, usually big rocks, but some-times logs or ledges give the same damming effect. Some such barrier is necessary or fish simply could not live in these areas where the current is moving at seventeen to twenty feet per second.

When the sunken fly is used, it must be large—6, 3X long to 2, 2X long, and it must have hackle enough to give it life and movement. Since the fly is not going to be in the area of the hold more than one or two seconds, it must be large enough to be seen, and must look live enough to be taken.

In most cases, even with a weighted nymph, a Hi-D line is necessary, and a stout leader of not over four feet long is a must. By stout, I mean no smaller than .010 inches and .011 or .012 is better. When fish in such lies see something that appears edible and of worthwhile size go swirling by, they swing over, seize it, and immedi-ately wheel back behind their barrier. This grab-and-go technique puts a tremen-

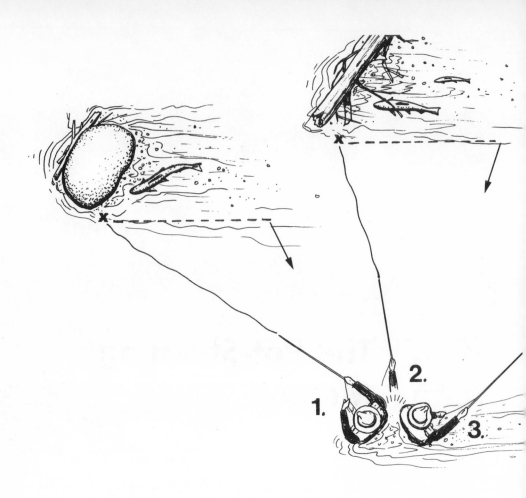

dous shock on the leader; I have had two-pounders in such places snap a six-pound-test leader like grocery twine.

The reason is that such spots must be fished with a short, tight line, and with the rod usually pointing down the line. The sudden jerk of a lunging fish, with nothing to absorb the shock, will break leaders three times the strength of the trout's dead weight.

The cast is *always* short; twenty feet is maximum. That means, with an eight-foot rod and a four-foot leader, only eight feet of line beyond the rod tip. The position one stands to fish this short line is very important. One must find a spot where the fly can be steered through the *edge* of the pocket under complete control. Whether that means your position is above, below, or alongisde the pocket often has to be determined by trial and error.

When in position, cast just beyond the upper edge of the pocket; the rod finishes low and parallel to the water, pointing to the spot where the fly entered. Swing your rod tip downstream very quickly in an attempt to keep it pointing at the spot

X   CAST TARGET

-- -- NYMPH PATH

← PICKUP POINT

Various types of pot shooting—upstream, across stream, and downstream

where the fly is at all times, thus, the tight line and "steering" technique. It works because the current is so mixed up in such areas that the trout is unable to make a split-second determination of whether something is drifting naturally or not. He has only an instant to make up his mind; it is now or never. Since trout in such areas feel very secure, they will make more mistakes than will trout in quieter waters, and we fishermen need all the cooperation we can get.

Once the fly clears the lower edge of the pocket, it is picked up instantly and "shot" back to the upper edge, and this is repeated over and over, fifteen to twenty times if no strike is forthcoming. This is where the method gets its name.

I cannot recall ever taking a trout of less than two pounds by this method, and three- and four-pounders are more common in such waters here in the West than they are in quieter waters. Before the Canyon section of the Madison below Hebgen Dam was blocked by a slide in the 1959 earthquake, and thus became covered by Quake Lake, the pockets in that raging torrent held trout that *averaged* four pounds, and there were many larger ones. I have had fish in those pockets snap twelve-pound-test leaders in one rolling lunge after taking the big No. 4 stonefly nymph.

Although it offers what I consider the best chance of consistently getting into fish of two pounds up, the method has its drawbacks. One may be getting to the river itself, for such rapids and cascades are often located in steep, rocky canyons, difficult to get into and out of. Then, once you have attained the river, you may find that you cannot wade it at all, and thus may be unable to reach any of the pockets without casting a fairly long line across currents moving in excess of ten miles per hour. Also, it *can* be dangerous! I have known of several anglers who were badly injured or killed by wading beyond their depth in such waters.

Sometimes, you can take fish by casting thirty or more feet to such pockets. You will lose the more precise control that much shorter casts allow, but by working each such pocket with twenty to forty casts and drifts you may be able to take the fish that will usually be there. I would always advise this approach if one is not absolutely sure of his wading ability. A good thing to remember is that paraphrase of the old Air Force saying about old-bold pilots: there are old waders, and there are bold waders, but there are no old, bold waders. It is a good thing to remember.

Size and color—and style— of fly are more important than accurate representation. For this reason, the old standby Wooly Worm is hard to beat for pot-shooting. Black, brown, and olive green seem to work better than other colors although there are times when yellow or orange bodies will work. I am unable to explain why this is so. Barred Rock (grizzly) hackle is my first choice because it adds more life and is highly visible. Life and visibility are the two major requirements for a fly used in this method; size, of course, helps visibility.

This is one of my favorite methods, partly because of the size of fish it regularly produces, and partly because such fish are seldom bothered by the regular run of fly-fishers. Invariably, when I see someone fishing this method, they will be using a floating line and a long leader. Sometimes it will work. For more consistent results with larger trout you must get your fly down to him, not ask him to come up for it. Always try to accommodate your trout with any method. This principle works almost as well with fish as it does with people.

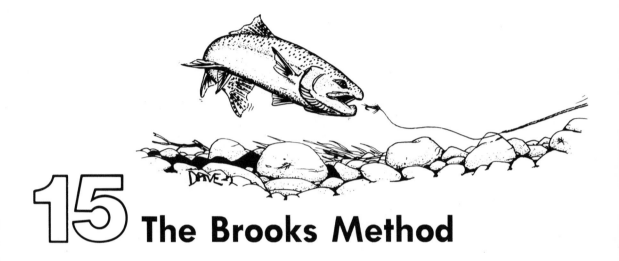

15 The Brooks Method

ALTHOUGH THIS IS ONE OF THE MOST WIDELY APPLICABLE METHODS TO THE FAST-water runs of the West and Northwest, I have never seen it used except by persons to whom I have taught it, or others who have picked it up from people I have taught. That is why the method bears my name. Perhaps 80 percent of my nymph fishing is with this method. The reasons are that the conditions required are in streams close by, and it is the most consistent method I know for taking trout from a pound up.

I must tell you here that many people to whom I have taught it do not like it. They do not like the tackle required and many are not at ease in the strong currents where this method must be used. Most of these people agree with my estimate of its effectiveness but they find it not pleasant to do. Also, many never acquire the skill and timing of the strike. Others become furious at the many missed strikes and the frustration drives them to other methods. No one I know, with the possible exception of John Rose, will fish it as much and with as much dedication as I do. Yet there are several, like Bob Holmes, who are as good or better at the method than I am.

There are miles and miles of water near my home that favor this method. These deep, rocky, very fast runs are more common on some streams than any other type of water. The Yellowstone from below Tower Falls to the mouth of Yankee Jim Canyon is almost continuously fast, deep, and full of big rocks. The Madison, from Hebgen Dam to the mouth of the Bear Traps, nearly a hundred miles, is nearly all of this nature. Henry's Fork, in Box Canyon and other areas, has several miles of such water that harbor very large fish—up to fifteen pounds.

My favorite stretch of all, though, is the Madison in Yellowstone Park, the section known locally as "behind the Barns," and which was once known officially as Riverside. Here the Park Service has a gauging station and at one time had a weather station.

It is just ten miles from my home to the end-of-road parking area on the banks of Hole Number Two, and I can be there in twenty minutes. Usually, I will walk downstream some distance and fish back. Some days I will only go as far as Hole Number Three, three-eighths of a mile downstream, and the last of the locally numbered "holes," which are, in fact, deep, fast runs. But I may decide to go to the last of the fast-water runs, at the beginning of the Beaver Meadows stretch, some three miles from Hole Number Two. It takes a full day to fish back to the car from here, if one does his work properly.

Sometimes I will follow the fishermen's paths along the stream, but mostly, I will stick to the old road, now closed to vehicle traffic, which goes to the meadow section. The road is shorter, cutting across the sweeping curves of the river. It travels the lodgepole forest, until of a sudden, you come out on a high bank with the meadows before you, the river on your right. It runs straight beside you for a quarter mile, then bends sharply across your path to bring an end to the old road, and a beginning (if you fish back upstream) of some of the finest fast-water fishing in the country.

The surroundings are exceptionally lovely. The meadows widen quickly to a width of a half mile. On the high bluffs flanking them, marking the limits of the stream in centuries past, the lodgepoles stand dense and black. Beyond, the mountains loom in all directions. They are frosted with snow in spring and fall, pinkish and beige below the snow to the timberline. On the left, to the west, the Henry's Lake Range, on the eastern base of which my home sits, circles to the north, jagged and uneven. The peaks have satisfying names: Targhee, highest in the range, Baldy, Lionhead, Sheep, Coffin, and White Peak. To the north the river cuts through them in what used to be the famous Madison Canyon, now blocked by a rock slide and covered by Quake Lake. Beyond here the Madison and Gallatin ranges and their subranges, the Tepees, Hildgards, and lesser ones, blend to form the spine dividing the watersheds of these two great rivers. On the right (east) Mount Holmes, Dome Mountain, The Crags, and Crowfoot Ridge stretch to the limits of vision, enclosing a great basin through which the Madison flows to Hebgen Lake and beyond.

The meadow grass grows tall—a deep, rich, waist-high green sea, interspersed with lighter green willows in the spring. In the fall, my favorite time, the meadows are tawny gold against the black of the lodgepoles, and the willows brilliant yellow, like splotches of sunlight. The river is a wide blue ribbon winding along the base of the bluffs, becoming green where beds of weeds flourish in the slower sections and along the edges of the channels.

It is the channels you must fish, for these boulder-filled cuts have the depth and current barriers to provide holds for trout up to five pounds, though the average is only one and a half. The water is fast, the current in the runs moves at a speed of six to eight miles per hour. The long riffles that separate the runs are also fast—too fast to allow trout to live in them, except for the rare boulders or potholes that slow the current. These are resting spots and one will occasionally find trout of three pounds in such potholes or behind the even scarcer boulders. But the fish is only passing through; he does not live there, and it is not usually worth your time to search out and fish such places.

The tackle one must use to fish the deep runs does not appeal to some—the light-tackle people especially. Such fishing requires a rod of eight or nine feet to control the drift, and with enough backbone to raise thirty feet of deeply sunken line and a weighted nymph and hurl it back upstream without false casting. False casting a heavy weighted nymph is a form of Russian roulette with eyes and ears as stakes.

Such fast, boulder-filled water is stonefly water just about any place it is found in trout streams. Therefore, the nymph should be large and well weighted. Fish in such waters will not move far from behind their boulders or from their bottom depressions to seize even a large nymph as it sweeps by. It has been my experience that they will not move at all to take a small nymph.

Trout survive, as they have for millions of years, by balancing the expenditure of energy to acquire food with the size or food value of the item of food they are after. Of course, this is not a conscious act; it is an instinct, and over the millions of years they have existed, those trout that had this instinct survived, those that did not have it died. Thus, by the process of "natural selection," all wild trout that have come down through the ages have this instinctive balancing of the desire for food against the amount of energy required to obtain it.

When a trout in such currents darts from behind his boulder, or lifts up from a bottom depression to seize a nymph, he is instantly slammed with the full force of what actually amounts to a moving wall of water. That water will be moving, in some cases, at twelve or more feet per second. It will thrust the trout downstream several feet in the half second or so it takes him to reach and grab the nymph speeding by. The instant he has secured the nymph, the trout will whirl sharply upstream to swim back to the protection of his lie. It is then, if his line is under control, that the angler will feel the strike, a hard, fierce jerk. The answering strike must also be fast and hard or you will not hook your fish.

Thus, the basis of the method is getting a large artificial down deep enough for the trout to see it and want to take it, and under enough control to be able to feel and hook the fish if he does take it.

All currents moving at a good speed over irregular bottoms cause turbulence that beats air into portions of the water, which being less dense than the surrounding water, tend to thrust upward to the surface. These updwellings, as they are called, further complicate the angler's attempt to keep his fly deep by lifting it, and the line and leader, toward the surface. The fast-sinking or Hi-D line, short leader, and heavily weighted fly combine not only to give a very fast sink rate, to get the fly to the bottom quickly, but also to help keep it there.

The leaders I use are four to six feet long, never longer, and the tip will be from .010 to .012 inches. They have to be short in order for the updwellings not to lift them too far and they have to be strong in order not to break on the strike. If you come up hard on a three-pound or heavier trout broadside in fast water, finer leaders will snap like cobwebs. It is not a matter of sporting or unsporting applica-

A very deep powerful run, calling for the giant stonefly nymph and the Brooks method.

tion; it is a matter of fact. I see no point in fishing if the intent is not to hook and hold the fish. Otherwise, one would not even need fish to fish for. Any water would do.

Stonefly water in my part of the country means *Pteronarcys* or *Acroneuria*, more often the former. Therefore, artificial nymphs from size 4, 4X long, to size 8, 3X long, are used. The larger the nymph—as long as it does not greatly exceed the size of the natural—the easier it will be for the trout to see, and be inclined to take. Some anglers hereabouts go as large as No. 2, 2X long. Actually, that is the same shank length as the size 4, 4X long, and it is easier to hook fish on the smaller size because the wire is finer and the barb smaller. It all helps.

In other areas of the country, smaller genera of stoneflies are found in such waters. These might be *Perla, Taeniopteryx, Arcynopteryx,* or other even smaller ones, and one must determine what nymphs are in his water in order to fish a representative artificial. Also, in lesser depths and current speeds, a different method of achieving the dead-drift might be used.

In all probability the larger the artificial nymph, the less accurate the imitation should be, and while color, form, and size must be fairly accurate, a suggestion of other features might be better than a detailed representation. For my own use, since my underwater studies have shown that live nymphs stay right side up whether swimming or drifting, I feel better with a nymph that has no distinctive back or belly, and one that has hackle completely around the body, rather than being bearded underneath or sticking out the sides. Fifteen years of unqualified success with nymphs so designed and fished in fast water have strengthened my belief in this form of tie.

In my method of fishing the nymph, one casts upstream but *fishes* down. The purpose of the upstream cast is to give the nymph time to sink before one commences to attempt to control and fish it. For this reason, the position for the first cast in any stretch should be some yards upstream of any suspected fish. You will work down to him on succeeding casts.

I call it five-phase fishing. Phase one is position. When I first start to fish a run, I position myself about twenty feet upstream of the commencement of deeper water, and about five feet back from the edge of the channel.

The first cast, phase two, will be upstream about fifteen feet and about six feet out from where I am standing. This will, with an eight-foot rod and a four-foot leader, require about ten feet of line past the rod tip. If one tossed a loose block of wood (instead of the fly) to this upstream spot, it should come downcurrent and reach a spot six feet or so opposite. Your fly will do the same, except it will be on the bottom. At this point, you will have fourteen feet of line and leader out, plus your rod, yet the fly is only six feet away. So you will have a lot of slack to deal with to bring the fly under control.

The time from when the fly hits the water until it comes opposite is phase three, sinking phase. Your fly *should* be on the bottom when it reaches this point.

This leads to phase four, the control phase. As fly and line move downstream, the rod tip is kept pointed above the spot where the line enters the water, and is also lifted so that only a slight droop is in the line between the rod tip and the water. On

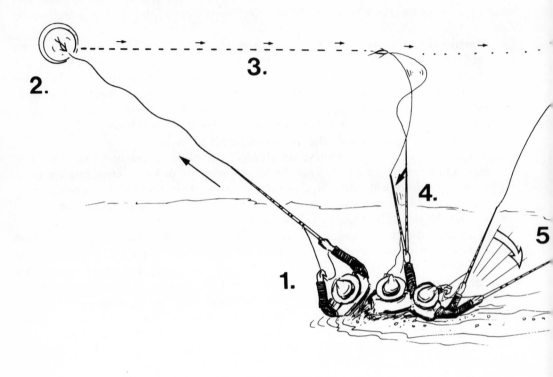

this first short cast, a lift of the rod tip to a point only just above the waist will take care of the slack. On a cast of thirty to forty feet, the rod will be pointed straight up and the arms stretched high overhead, just to accomplish the same thing. On these longer casts, when you are in the just described position, you are helpless if a fish hits. This is another reason you always start fishing well upstream of the expected lie of *any* fish.

Phase five is the fishing phase, from a point slightly downstream of straight across until the fly comes straight below. As the fly and line move on downstream, the angler pivots slightly to face across and down. At the same time, the rod tip, always aimed above the spot where the line enters the water (even when pointing straight up), is lowered slowly and swung downstream. The objective is to keep only a slight droop in the visible part of the line, and to keep moving the rod tip *as necessary* to maintain the droop. Too tight a line will cause the fly to lift due to current pull. Too much slack will cause missed strikes. One must sail between Scylla and Charybdis. It requires great concentration and an understanding of exactly what one is trying to do.

When the line comes straight downstream, do not pick up and recast immediately. Wait at least five seconds. The reason for this delay is to allow the bow in the

A five-phase drawing of the Brooks method, showing position, the cast, the sinking nymph, control of slack, and fishing out the cast

line and leader to straighten. No matter how skillful the angler, that bow will always be there. This is because the fly is traveling in the slower bottom current, while the line and leader cuts through the faster currents to the surface. The bow will be four to eight feet in depth, from fly to apex of the bow. There is no way to eliminate it and still have the fly along the bottom where it belongs.

It is this bow that causes the hooking problem. The bow does not have to be completely straightened out on the strike to hook the fish. If the jerk by the angler is *fast* enough, the resistance of the water to the line will cause the hook to be driven home. In effect, it is something like having a rope in your hand that is passed around a pulley, brought back and looped around your own ankle. A pull on the rope with your hand will probably not upset you, but a strong jerk would.

If one can always strike upstream, the chances of hooking are better simply because of increased water resistance. On a downstream strike, the rod and line hand must move through greater distances to set the hook.

This is two-handed striking; one hand throwing the rod tip to one side, the other snatching the line through the stripping guide in the opposite direction. There must always be three or four feet of slack between the reel and the line hand so as not to impede this violent stripping action. As you can see, it is also two-handed fishing;

This is the way slack is controlled on a long cast, using the Brooks method.

the line must be strongly held in the fingers of the line hand at all times once the drift is started.

Line is *not* retrieved with the line hand during the drift. Control is maintained by the raising and lowering of the rod tip, and your arms, if necessary. You raise the rod tip (and arms on long casts) as the line and fly move downstream *toward* you. You lower the rod tip and arms as the line and fly move *away* from you, trying to keep exactly the same slight droop in the line between rod tip and water.

The pickup and recast, without false casting, is difficult for some to learn, mostly because of the ingrained habits of normal casting. When one is casting short, twenty to thirty feet, rod butt to fly, pickup and recast is not too much of a problem. But when you have thirty or more feet of line *past* the rod tip, the ordinary pickup will not work with the fast-sinking or Hi-D line and the weighted nymph.

Let us return to phase two, casting phase, a moment. As stated, one starts with a short cast, about fifteen feet upstream and five or six feet out. Make this same cast and drift three to five times before lengthening line. After each series of three to five casts and drifts, strip off about five more feet of line and commence another series. Do not change position until you have got out all the line you can control. The amount will vary with different anglers. For me, the maximum is about thirty-five feet of line past the rod tip. With a four-foot leader and eight-foot rod, this is a cast of forty-seven feet. At this point, I will have completed about five series of casts and drifts, each series commencing about three feet farther upstream and the same distance out. A total of twenty-five to thirty casts and drifts will be involved. Thorough coverage of the bottom is the aim. Once you have reached the limits of good line control, it is time to retrieve all but ten feet of line past the rod tip and move ten or so feet downstream to take up a new phase one position. Here the whole series is repeated, followed by another move down, until the run is covered.

Now, back to casting once we have considerable line out, say thirty feet past the rod tip. For right-handed casters on the left side of the stream (looking downstream, as banks or sides are defined), the pickup and cast will be backhanded. Here is how it is done. After the line has come straight below, and after you have waited the additional five seconds for the line-leader bow to straighten, you are ready. At this point, you should have pivoted to face slightly across and down, your rod should be low over the water and parallel to it, and everything—casting arm, rod, line, and leader—should be in a straight line, downcurrent. The line, leader, and fly will be sunken, and this must be overcome in making the cast.

Raise the entire rod, keeping it parallel to the water, until it is shoulder high. This will lift *most* of the line from the water, and this move is the key to all else.

At the same time the rod hand moves, the line hand, extended as far toward the stripping guide as possible, moves also, keeping its relation to the rod hand. The instant the rod comes shoulder high *and while it is still moving*, strip down and toward the hip with the line hand. As the strip starts, the rod is swung, backhanded with a straight arm, out over the water and upstream. The rod tip does *not* come upright or over. The cast is like a tennis backhand, with the rod almost parallel to the water throughout. In essence, this is a backhanded level cast with a single haul.

In order for the fly not to come straight upstream, the swing of the rod is stopped with the tip pointing just upstream of straight across. The line hand releases the line at this point, and the line will continue to carry upstream at about a forty-five-degree angle.

As in all methods, it requires practice to get the line and fly to go where you want them, and to do this properly requires timing that can only be learned through practice. The beauty of this method of casting is that it requires only one cast to place the fly in position for the next drift and that the hook never comes within twenty feet of the head at any time. We use many weighted flies in our western fast-water fishing, and every year at least a dozen persons in this area hook themselves about the head because they cast in the normal back-and-forth manner.

When fishing this, or any fast-water method, always be sure that your feet are planted solidly at all times, so that the motions of casting—or striking—do not allow the current to knock you off your feet. I like to face about twenty degrees downstream of straight across, plant my feet and leave them planted, pivoting at the waist rather than moving my feet.

The casting for a right-handed caster on the right side of the stream is easier than the backhanded method. Here the drift of the fly takes the place of the normal backcast. When the drift is finished, and the five-second wait is over, the angler raises rod and arm shoulder high, then makes a powerful horizontal forward cast upstream, stopping the rod tip just after it passes the straight-across position. The line is stripped when the cast is started and released when the rod swing stops.

Casting is very difficult to describe, and this cast particularly so. But once learned, it saves much energy and is far safer than any other that I know when casting weighted nymphs.

Many persons are skeptical of both this method of fishing and the just described form of casting, especially when they see the water in which the fishing is to be done. They usually require some convincing.

In the fall of 1972, Art Flick came out to do some fishing in this area. I had not met Art, but when Nick Lyons called to say he was coming and asked if I would show him around, I was more than happy to do so. Since I felt that I might need some backing, I enlisted the help of Bob Holmes.

When Art and his two friends, John Hoeko and Judd Weisberg, arrived, we were in the depths of a very cold snap. Since dry-fly fishing would not be profitable before two in the afternoon, Bob and I took the easterners down to the Beaver Meadows to teach them my method of nymph fishing.

As I was explaining the method, Art kept glancing at the raging fast water and back at me. His face had that look that fishermen get when someone is expounding on their favorite method.

I had taken the water temperature; it was only 46 degrees and when I explained that it would have to reach 52 degrees before we could expect any action, Art's face took on a resigned look. When I said that we wouldn't take any decent fish before eleven-thirty, I thought he was going to leave. Bob, snickering throughout my explanation, did not help the situation. Even when I explained that we had come early so that the men could get in some practice before the fish started taking, I could see no one believed me.

Art picked up the method quickly, as did Judd and John, laboring under Bob's watchful eye. By the time we had reached Hole Number Three on the way back to

A large weighted nymph, Hi-D line, short leader, and the Brooks method are required in this deep surging run.

the car, Art had received some strikes, but had failed to hook the fish. He took heart when I told him that these had been small fish that always commence feeding sooner than their larger brethren.

At eleven-thirty I checked the temperature; it was exactly 52 degrees, so I called to Art, waist deep in the stream, that we could expect action at any time.

Action we got. My voice had barely died away when a two-pound rainbow exploded from the stream, Art's nymph in its jaw. Art lost that fish; after a series of splendid acrobatics, it came unstuck. But he landed two even larger in the next ten minutes and missed several good hits. John, Judd, and Bob were also taking fish, and at one time all four had fish of over a pound on at once.

As we headed up to the Firehole and Iron Creek for dry-fly fishing that afternoon, Art confessed that he had had little faith in the method. "That first rainbow changed my thinking," he said "and the next two, coming so quickly, made a believer out of me. There are some big rainbows and some fast water on the Delaware that I'm going to work your method on next year. I want you to know you have a convert, that you've taught an old dog some new tricks."

Art was sixty-nine when this happened. He was a dyed-in-the-wool dry-fly man. Yet, he was willing to give the method a try because I had convinced him it would work. I hope I have convinced my readers also.

16 The Leftovers

ONE COULD SAY WITH ALMOST PERFECT ASSURANCE THAT NEARLY ANY METHOD OF fishing the nymph will work at times. But since consistent results are what we are after, we will have better success if we use the method that presents *that* nymph in a most natural manner.

Nearly all the mayfly, caddis fly, midge, and blackfly nymphs and larvae need to be imitated at two stages in their underwater life: the developing stage, which may last from three months to more than three years, and the hatching stage, which may last only a minute or two. Stonefly nymphs and alderfly larvae (hellgrammite and fish fly) cannot be successfully imitated during actual hatching, since they crawl out rather than emerge. Yet, two methods can be used to imitate the developing form—crawling the artificial along the bottom and dead-drifting it. The water type and current speed will dictate which method you *can* use.

By this time one should be aware that all the methods and variations in the preceding chapters do not cover the entire range of possibilities, because large stretches of water were involved in most cases. But there are many tight holds and spot lies that will require special and specific methods, and there are specialized water types that will require special handling.

In certain precipitous mountain streams, a situation often exists where the nymph must be dead-drifted deep in fast water but where a sinking line cannot be used because many boulders or logs, or both, reach up near to, or protrude above, the surface. In Colorado and California, this is a rather common situation and the anglers there have learned to deal with it in a satisfactory manner.

This type water would be a run (not a rapid) with a boulder-rubble bottom. The current is not as fast as it appears, in spite of the foaming and swirling around the protruding logs or boulders. The reason is that the boulders themselves act as a series of check dams, slowing, diverting, and sometimes reversing the current. Thus, the floating line that must be used to avoid constant entanglement is not as big a drawback as it might appear.

The most successful of the anglers who use the following method use a full-floating line, a long, fairly fine leader, an unweighted nymph—and weight the leader as needed to keep the fly near the bottom.

Since the conditions require a compromise in tackle, there are also pluses and minuses in its use. Since the floating line is easier to see than a sunken line would be, control and striking are easier. But the lump of lead on the leader rules out normal casting unless you enjoy getting thumped behind the ear. The cast has to be nearly horizontal, and arm and rod are swung in a slow, smooth arc. Timing is difficult; even the most proficient at this method get an uncomfortable jerk now and then when they mistime a direction change.

One can fish up and across, across, or down and across as needed to cover the water. The line is mended as necessary to maintain a drag-free float, and on short casts the fly can actually be steered near and around boulders, covering the best lies quite precisely. For these reasons, this can be and often is a very effective method. As in nearly all nymph methods, detecting the strike and hooking the fish are the biggest problems.

The method is almost entirely dead-drift, although some who use the method also hand retrieve during the drift. However, in really mixed-up currents where protruding rocks are plentiful, trying to do this while steering the fly, mending the line, and watching and feeling for indications of a strike can give you the feeling of juggling a handful of marbles while making love.

Fishing the nymph in spot lies will require a method suited to the exact spot; what works here will not work there, and each situation will require a different analysis and approach. The angler is on his own here, but should keep in mind that whatever method it takes to do the job is the one that should be used.

Ray Bergman wrote of taking a particularly difficult trout from a specific spot by using a very different form of nymph fishing. He tied a large dipsey sinker on the tippet of his leader and put the nymph on a short dropper a few inches above. He then lowered this rig gently into the trout's lie and activated it by tiny slackenings and tightenings of the leader. He got his trout.

The above method smacks of bait fishing but the nymph fisher who wishes to do well should remember that his artificial does imitate "bait," and that he will have more consistent success if he fishes it as though it were a live nymph. And if, like many, he feels he must catch fish to succeed, then he will have to use many unorthodox methods.

Many anglers do feel they have to catch fish in order to prove themselves. I am luckier than most, in that during the years I spent in Alaska there were a total of over thirty days when I caught and released over two hundred *pounds* of fish, plus scores of days when the total was over a hundred pounds. Thus, when I left there, I was forever relieved of the need to feel I *had* to catch fish. Not many anglers are so fortunate.

This fast, boulder-lined run is stonefly water, but one must use a floating line to avoid entanglement. Fishing it requires one of the special methods covered in this chapter.

No criticism is meant or implied here. Although nonanglers tend to lump us all together as a bunch of nuts (maybe we are) all from the same tree, the fact is we are all individuals with different hopes, fears, skills, talents, and goals. The most felicitous expression of this that I know was that used by John Waller Hills in *A History of Fly Fishing for Trout*. He was talking about five greats of the Waltonian era, Walton, Cotton, Barker, Venables, and Franck. He called them the most diversified crew that ever embarked in the same boat and said, "Had they all met together, which thank heaven they never did, there is no subject on which they could have agreed except fishing, and there would have been broken heads over that."

So, one not need feel guilty about any method of fishing the artificial nymph. Look on those special fish as a challenge and go after them. There is great satisfaction in taking a very good fish from a particularly difficult lie.

For two years now I have been after a big brown in the Firehole. He holds under an undercut bank in four feet of water. There is a deep notch in the bank at the head of his lie that causes an eddy that defeats any attempt to reach him by the natural drift. A huge tree stands just back from the notch, and its limbs sweep low out over the water. I have not been able to come up with a taking method of getting a nymph to him *yet*.

Half-sunken logs and drifts are top holding spots for fish and very tough to fish. Almost every one of them presents a different problem. All require some study before one attempts to fish them.

In some areas one can fish a full-floating line, fine leader, and deliver the cast from below the drift. As the nymph—and line—float down toward the face of the drift or log, raise the rod tip to control slack. When the tip of the line reaches the drift face, wait one or two seconds longer for the fly to get back under the drift. Then snap the upraised rod tip sharply down—a modified roll cast. In most cases, this will pluck the fly from under the drift without hanging it up. Then one can make a normal backcast and deliver the nymph back upstream to start a new float. Cover the area under the drift or log thoroughly and use weight on the leader or under the fly body to get the fly down. As always, use a two-handed strike, using the line hand to control the strength of the strike. If you come up firmly against a fish, let some line slip through your fingers.

The disadvantage of the above method is apparent. Once you have hooked your fish, you are fighting him *over* the log or drift and everything is in his favor. You are on your own in handling such fish but I prefer to slack off completely until I can work my way upstream above him, then tighten up and start over. You will still lose some good fish but I can guarantee a thrill each time you hook one by this method.

You can also fish such places on a long line from above. Current speed will usually dictate whether a full-floating, sink-tip, or full-sinking line must be used. You must use a line—and fly—that will have the fly deep under the log or drift when it gets there.

Sometimes an across-and-down drift can be made so that the fly swings under the obstruction. This requires good eyesight and timing when using a sunken line, but often is very effective. The above is easier to accomplish with a full-floating line but somewhat less effective. Although in both methods one will do better with an artificial that represents a natural found in the area, fish in such locations usually feel quite secure and will sample even very unusual offerings if presented naturally.

Several years ago, I developed a method by accident that has proven very good in such places, though I must admit I feel a little silly each time I use it. I had been trying by several methods to get a nymph under a large half-sunken log across a fast-water stretch of a small stream. The rush and flow of the current made it difficult; a floating line rushed down so swiftly that it snatched the fly up near the surface. With a sunken line I could not tell where my fly was. I had returned to using the floating line and decided to try a straight downstream cast *over* and beyond the log, then jerk back at the last split second to drop the fly just above the log with a little slack.

On the first attempt, the weighted nymph hit the log dead center with a clearly heard click, then bounced about two feet upstream, dropped, and sank. A nice trout had it the instant it got under the log. I had often used this method in my boyhood, with a floating bass bug, popping it against a log or tree stump to drop into the water. It had been deadly, but it had never occurred to me to use the technique with a nymph.

This little stream had (and has) dozens of such logs lying across it. My accidentally discovered method turned out to be very successful, for the trout averaged two pounds and they run much larger. What is this little stream? Don't ask.

If the fly isn't taken at once, when it gets back under the log, let it hang there on the end of the line. Hold the rod tip low, even touching the water, and move it slowly right and left, pausing at each side and in the center. Sometimes the hit will come after two minutes of such activity.

At first I was puzzled by the success of this method. I was sure no underwater insect would behave in this manner. I was wrong. A few of the smaller caddises, and a much greater number of midge and blackfly larvae, fasten themselves to rocks or wood underwater by strong, incredibly fine threads. When they feed, or for any reason decide to move, they simply unreel this silken thread a foot or more, letting the current carry them down, where they hang and swing, doing whatever it is they do. When they wish to return "home," they just reel themselves in.

All the above larvae are small to tiny and a small—14 to 18—artificial with a larva-like look works best. Bodies of cream, gray, tan, or black fur, slim and straight with a fuzzy thorax of brown or black, and a head of tying thread are all these simple patterns require.

There may be larger forms that hang in the current, although I do not know about them. Yet, a size 14 works more often for me than smaller sizes and a 12 will occasionally take fish when used in the above manner. I put a turn of partridge hackle on at the head of these two sizes.

→

In the open water, the Skues, Sawyer. Hewitt, Live Nymph, Upstream, Leisenring Lift, and Rising-to-the-Surface methods all will work at the proper time with the proper nymph. Fishing around the logs and drifts requires the special methods in this chapter.

One is somewhat limited to the methods he may use in such still waters as pools, ponds, and lakes. Yet, handling the nymph in still water is much easier than in moving water and control is much more precise. The real problem of fishing the nymph in ponds and lakes, other than the obvious one of identifying the nymphs therein, is in locating the fish. Once the fish is located, its position and actions along with knowledge of the live nymphs in the water will dictate the method to be used.

If mayflies are hatching, one matches the nymph, uses a full-floating line and long, fine leader, and attempts to simulate the actions of the preemergent nymph. If caddises are hatching (a much more likely prospect), one can use sinking lines, shorter leaders, and variations of the Rising-to-the-Surface or Leisenring Lift techniques. If midge or blackfly are hatching, the condition sometimes called the "smutting rise" will be taking place. This merely means that the trout are daintily sipping in the larvae in the meniscus or surface film. All dry-fly tackle except the fly is used and one tries to drop the tiny artificial at the proper spot ahead of the cruising fish.

It is when such activity is not taking place, when the underwater activities of the developing nymphs, larvae, and scud must be imitated, that the fisherman's job becomes quite complicated. Knowing where to fish in most lakes is more difficult knowledge to acquire than the same information in streams because the surface of a lake gives little or no clue to its underwater character.

Some lakes yield such information simply by limiting the spots where it is possible to fish the sunken fly. One such is Henry's Lake, just over the pass from my home, and perhaps the best fly-fishing lake in the entire country.

A combination of happy circumstances gives this lake its obliging nature. It is almost entirely spring fed; there are large springs in the bottom, and even the creeks running into it originate from springs. Thus, the temperature, oxygen content, and even its mineral richness are quite stable. It is shallow, its average depth about twelve feet. There is hardly any spot where one cannot get the fly to the bottom—if an open space in the weeds can be found. The weed beds are not the bother they might seem. The fisherman can only fish the lanes between them, but the fish prefer to move in these lanes. This puts the fish, when they are moving, in the only spots where the nymph can be fished.

The weeds are full of scuds and sow bugs, which are preyed upon by a green damselfly nymph, and nearly every knowledgeable angler that fishes this lake uses an imitation of one of the above. One does not need to know or identify any of them if he buys his nymph patterns locally.

The fish in this lake are mostly rainbow-cutthroat hybrids, cutthroats, and some few very large brook trout. The hybrids have been artificially created for the purpose of fast maturity. This, coupled with the stable conditions and the unbelievable amount of food, causes these fish to reach a very large size at an early age. How large? Up to eighteen pounds, but most are caught between two and six pounds. The really knowledgeable nympher will make consistent catches of large trout in Henry's Lake that seem not possible to persons who do not know it.

There was a doctor from Los Angeles who spent each June, July, and August at Henry's Lake from 1946 to 1970. In an interview that appeared in the Sunday supplement of a Los Angeles paper a few years back, the doctor made the statement that in those twenty-five years he had averaged over a hundred fish a summer above *five* pounds. The doctor is well known around the lake and no one doubts his account in the slightest. He used only three flies to accomplish his feat—a scud or shrimp imitation like Trueblood's Otter Shrimp, a green damselfly nymph, and a green-bodied Wooly Worm. These, and the Leech, are all the flies anyone needs for this lake.

The method of fishing is even more simple. One locates (in a boat) alongside a channel in the weeds, casts a long line, lets the nymph sink well down, and then hand-twist retrieves in what Nick Lyons calls "a slow, haunting rhythm." It is just about that simple in Henry's Lake, although there will be days there, as elsewhere, when no fish come to your fly, however well fished.

In most lakes one can depend on imitations of dragon and damselfly nymphs. If there are other insects in the lake these two predators almost surely will be also. One really does not need to know exactly what genera and species are there. If you have each type in three sizes and three colors (and you should), then you will be able to find one that will work. In dragonfly nymph patterns I would want brown, tan, and gray in sizes 4, 6, and 8, 2X long. In the damsel patterns I would want green, tan, and olive in sizes 6, 8, and 10, also 2X long. With that assortment I could handle most lakes.

I would feel better if I could locate some fish to fish to, but failing that, I would go to work with a fast-sinking or Hi-D line, a long leader to 3X, and my weighted nymphs. I would cast as far as I could, let sink, then use a fast hand-twist retrieve with now and then a short twitch. I would cover the area thoroughly and fish each cast back until the leader came through the rod tip. I would know when I found the fish because the hit to these nymphs fished in this manner is strong.

Fishing small deep pockets in pools calls for a method known as deep dibbling, although I think jigging conveys a better idea of the method. It is simply raising the nymph off the bottom and letting it flutter back. As nearly as possible the lift should be straight up, no more than a foot, followed by a smooth drop on a barely slack line. Move the rod tip a foot or so to one side after each drop. Don't ask me what this imitates, I don't know. But the method works often enough so that it must be based on some creature's actions. A nondescript nymph of medium size in brown, gray, or black will work as well as a good nymph imitation.

Pockets of quiet water around roots, boulders, along undercut banks, and along the edge of sunken logs are where this method works best, and that is good, because practically no other method can be used in such places.

There is a stretch of the Yellowstone below Gardiner but before Yankee Jim Canyon where this is the only method that works.

The water is deep, over nine feet in places. Great boulders the size of refrigerators stacked on each other form the bottom. The gradient here slackens sharply, and there is a sort of bench. It appears that the huge boulders were rolled down the steep slant of the river above by floods, and came to rest here. It boggles the imagination to conceive how much force was required to do this; many of these rocks will weigh over three tons.

There are pocket caverns down among these rocks that are six feet deep and often not much bigger across. There is some current above the pockets but only the faintest of eddies down in them.

A Hi-D line and short leader are used and the method is dibbling. You stand on a boulder and let your nymph sink to the bottom of one of these deep pocket holes. Then you dibble.

The mayfly nymphs in this area run small. Sizes 16 to 22 are required and *Baetis* is the genus. In fact, a size 18 Blue Dun wet will work just about as well as anything. But there is a lot of dibbling between strikes, whatever is used, and there is great variance in the size of fish hooked. They will run from seven inches to as many pounds. Your chances of hauling one of the bigger ones out are slim and none.

Variations in nymph methods are endless. Let your imagination run free and use whatever method water and bottom type require.

Do whatever needs to be done to get your artificial to the fish in a natural manner. Try not to become so enamored with any method that you become a one-method fisherman, but do use more the methods that work best on your waters. Your success ratio should tell if you have chosen correctly.

←
Gravel bottom and moderate current spell mayfly and caddis fly forms. The depth one fishes will dictate the type of line one must use, and sometimes the size of the fish.

17 Nymphing for Larger Trout

BOB HOLMES, WHO MAY BE THE BEST ALL-AROUND FLY-FISHERMAN I KNOW, SAYS THAT 90 percent of catching larger trout lies in locating them. Since Bob spends considerable time locating fish larger than three pounds—and catching them—he speaks from experience.

However, for most, larger trout would run somewhat smaller than Bob's definition, say, from one to three pounds. That size still requires some locating and it certainly requires more effort and planning to catch trout of this size than it does the ordinary run of fish.

In years gone by, I spent a good deal of time looking for and learning about trout in the middleweight class, and I have come to know something of their habits and habitat. Thus, it has become possible many times to fish for, and sometimes to catch, such trout without actually locating them. I now do it largely by fishing the nymph in those places where such trout *should* be.

One such place has been discussed, the deep, boulder-lined runs where the Brooks method is required. In the past fifteen years less than 5 percent of the trout I have caught in these runs have weighed less than a pound. In that time only about a half-dozen fish of under a pound have come from the run itself. I have caught several tiddlers of ten or so inches when I was letting my nymph dawdle in the shallow, slower water at the edge of the run, but most of the fish deep in the run have been over the one-pound size and this really is the major reason I fish them so much. I don't like to be bothered releasing smaller fish when the larger ones are available.

Because I talk and write mostly about larger trout, a good many persons think I am strictly a lunker fisherman. Not so. Though I aim my efforts at fish over a pound, I am not one who spends all his time searching for and stalking lunkers. For the purposes of this chapter and the book, then, larger trout means those over a pound, up to however big we can catch without making a career out of one fish.

The first thing that one should know about these middleweights is that they will not usually be in shallow water unless they are feeding. If one finds them in such places, the problem is greatly simplified, for a feeding fish is simply easier to catch if one takes good care not to spook him.

No, most of the time your fish will not be in the shallows. If there are pools in your area, then you *may* find your fish there, but these larger fellows will not be easy to spot even in pools. They like, and usually have, some sort of overhead cover, and it is this cover that we are really looking for.

In the deep fast runs, the overhead cover is merely light refraction; in these mixed-up currents the fish cannot see above the surface, and with a depth of three or more feet he feels safe. If he didn't, he wouldn't be there.

Other spots may be more obvious. Large logs in the water are always a definite possibility if there is some depth. Drift piles, clumps of roots, undercut banks; any form of overhead cover where there is some depth will generally hold a good fish if the spot is not located in a large area of generally shallow water.

Angling pressure will have a definite effect on fish location. The harder a sizable fish is fished for the more secure hold he will be in. Thus, in hard-fished streams, some very good spots may be barren or contain only small fish.

Each of the "single hold" spots just described requires a different method of handling the nymph (as well as the proper nymph). It is hardly possible to cover each such spot in a book, but it is possible to discuss fishing some of them.

There are occasional undercut bank sections only a few feet long, flanking long deep, smooth-bottomed runs, on both the Firehole and Upper Madison. One can never see the fish back under these banks, but they can be *heard* feeding at times if one approaches carefully. These spots are perfect for a type of fishing the nymph that is a variation of the bank-walking variation of the Continuous Drift method.

Position yourself about the center of this short undercut bank section, about eight feet back from the edge. Approach and getting into position must be done with a slow, soft, and careful tread. No stumbling, no heavy-footed jarring of the ground, no sound that will alert your fish can be allowed.

Your nymph must be one that is to be found in that area at that time of year. For the Firehole or Upper Madison, I use a size 10 Ida May (*Ephemerella grandis*) until mid-July, then switch to a *Siphlonurus* imitation for the rest of the season. Both artificials will be well weighted under the body. My leader will be six feet, not finer than 2X. The line doesn't matter, you won't be casting.

With arm and rod extended, and just the leader through the rod tip, one reaches up as far as possible and lowers the nymph into the water just past the edge of the bank. Let it sink about a foot, then try to move it downstream along the bank edge by slowly swinging the rod at as near current speed as you can manage. When you have "led" the fly as far down as you can without moving your feet, lift the nymph clear, swing it back up to the starting point, and repeat the process. This may have to be done twenty to thirty times before the fish will take. In effect, this is George

LaBranche's "artificial hatch" using a nymph instead of a dry fly.

If you do not take a fish by this method, do not say he is not there. You may have spooked him by your approach or by clumsy handling of the nymph. Go away quietly to return and try for him another day.

This repeated passing of a nymph past a suspected lie or holding place is one of the best methods for spot holds. A trout is not frightened, usually, of a nymph that acts strangely, if he has not been otherwise alerted. However, several bad passes in succession will tell him that something strange is going on, so, according to the dictum *Omne ignotum pro horrifico*, he will usually shrink back into his hold until things return to normal.

The above is about the best way to fish the nymph in spot lies, but sometimes, for unknown reasons, it will not work, even when you know there is a fish there. Then you must try the other methods, dibbling, letting the fly downstream on a tight line to hang and swing in the area, or any method you can think of to get the nymph to the fish without frightening him.

To my mind, the most difficult spots to fish the nymph, yet which often hold good fish, are fast-water drop-offs, where a ledge, declivity, a log in the stream bed, or a row of sunken boulders lying athwart the stream causes a digging action as the water pours over them. These obstructions do not reach the surface; and in addition to causing the digging of a deeper area just below them, they will cause a structured current, a fast upper layer moving over a much slower or even reversed bottom layer. Such structured currents play havoc with line and leader control.

Here one must allow the nymph to enter the drop-off with a calculated amount of slack, so that the nymph will linger in the deeper water for a few seconds. The longer, the better, of course, but not so much slack can be allowed as to prevent detection of the take. Here is another place where repeated placing of the fly in the same area must be done, not with the idea of creating an "artificial hatch" but with the hope that at least one cast will present the fly naturally. Whether one casts into the area from below, above, or alongside is a matter of choice; I often fish into such areas from all sides, hoping to get at least one short drag-free drift that the fish will see. I consider such spots to be more challenging than any other type hold.

The first of such spots I ever fished was on the Middle Yuba in California in 1947. The current sped down a long steep, shallow slant and was squeezed between a rock and a rock wall just where it dropped over a foot-high ledge. There was a deep pocket of quieter water beneath the fast overriding current tongue. The look of the place just spelled fish.

I had been attempting to get my wet fly into the pocket with a natural drift for several minutes from several points, when a teen-age fly-fisherman came slopping up and dunked his fly into the area just in front of me. He immediately caught a fish, then another and another. Then with a sneering, superior smile, he moved on upstream.

It had been obvious to me that the youngster knew this stretch of water very well, so I moved over to the spot from which he had fished, and cast into the center of the current tongue with a short line as he had done. The fly was almost immediately pulled out of the current by the tight line, and started to circle upstream in a backcurrent alongside the main current. My fly was then taken and I also took another fish a few casts later.

This weed-bed-filled stretch calls for a floating line and small nymphs. It is very difficult to fish by any sunken fly method, yet holds very large trout.

I returned to the area several times at later dates and by trying from all sides found that one had to stand in the same place and fish in exactly the same manner as the youth had in order to get any action. I expect that youngster never did know what a favor he had done me.

The following year, I found a similar spot on the Gros Ventre in Jackson's Hole. Here a concrete roadbed had been built across the stream on the bottom in a very fast stretch. The water pouring over the lower edge had created a pothole and plunge pool. The water was racing swiftly over the roadbed, and the area just below was a turbulent, churning maelstrom. I could see dark green water back under the lower edge of the roadbed and knew that spelled depth.

Using a floating line, I cast the weighted No. 10 Brown Hackle straight up into the smooth torrent racing over the roadbed. As the fly came back, I raised the rod tip and stripped swiftly to control slack.

I saw the dark blob of my fly drop into the churning currents off the edge of the roadbed and the largest non-steelhead trout I had up to then seen took it with a savage rolling lunge. He at once fled back into the undercut beneath the roadbed and the leader parted on the rough edge of the concrete. I have never forgotten the spectacle of his huge dark body rolling in the foam as he curved and went down with my fly and the memory has kept me searching such places ever since.

The Firehole has several places where its bedrock bottom has dropped away, and the irresistible power of the current has created potholes and plunge pools, some quite large. I fish them often and have found that the fish will be lying in different spots, each according to his standing in the community, and one must fish from all points of the compass and cover the water thoroughly in order to be successful. In this form of nymph fishing for larger trout, study the problem from all angles and fish the area from all angles. You may find a spot and method that works after a dozen others have failed. Success is what we are after, but it is the failures that keep us coming back.

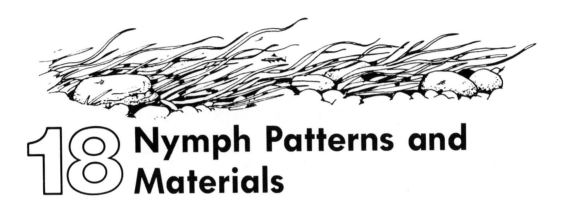

18 Nymph Patterns and Materials

THE TWO DOZEN OR SO PATTERNS LISTED AND DESCRIBED HERE ARE MERELY A GENERAL selection of several of each—imitative, suggestive, and impressionistic.

The instructions for tying and the materials used are general, also, partly because there are few standardized patterns, but mainly because the result is what counts and not the materials nor the method of tying.

Some flytiers express horror at using anything but fur for tying nymph bodies; others go to the other extreme and use rubber, plastic, and other synthetics such as flat nylon monofilament. No matter what material is used, if it is a little out of the ordinary, it will be hard to find.

Like Dave Whitlock, who mentions this in *Art Flick's Master Fly-Tying Guide*, I find many good items for fly-tying in yarn and sewing shops, and I am very fond of the fine fuzzy yarns of many, and even variegated, colors one can find in the larger yarn shops. Some of these are blended with angora and acrylics; and in my opinion are equal to the finest hair and fur combinations the tier can blend himself.

One of the best items I have found in sewing shops is gold and silver metallic threads made by the Dritz company. These are finer than the finest oval tinsels and are far stronger, as well as being much cheaper. These threads are made in exactly the same manner as oval tinsels, except they are not flattened but remain round. They come in several diameters, but I find the .010 inch diameter satisfactory for most purposes. You can also get various kinds of tinsel and Mylar tubing in such places, along with buttonhole twist threads, which make excellent ribbing material.

Nylon monofilament sewing thread is another item one can find in sewing shops; a spool of .0045-inch smoke-colored mono will cost about forty cents, and it will make several hundred of the best 6X tippets you have ever used. The brand most avail-,able is Sew-Gude by the Gudebrod Brothers Silk Co. of Philadelphia. It is called colorless (not "clear") and is almost invisible in water.

Hobby shops offer items for the flytier that cannot be found elsewhere. Since oval copper tinsel became extinct, I have been using .010-inch soft copper wire obtainable at hobby shops, where you can also get this same wire anodized in red, green, yellow, wine, and other colors for ribbing material. Hobby shops also carry a wide variety of glues and cements that the tier can use.

Hooks are a problem wherever you try to obtain them. Although most tiers have apparently resigned themselves to using Mustad hooks because they are most readily available, I do not like them because they are made of softer wire and thus are made of larger wire than the same size hooks of English make.

Most knowledgeable nymph fishers prefer to use finer wire hooks, even dry-fly hooks, in order to assure easier hooking on the strike, and use lead wire under the body to get the artificial to sink. This is the approach I use, and this brings up another point: you can get spools of lead solder or fuse wire from electric supply stores at about one-third the price that fly material houses charge. It is available in spools of one-quarter to one pound per spool, and in sizes ranging from .012 to .040 inches, and if you buy direct from a shop in your area, you will also save postage, which is considerable these days.

For blending fur colors for dubbing, there are two methods, the wet and the dry. Both are for blending large quantities of fur and are not suitable for the occasional tier.

In the wet method, the fur is placed in a pot of water and as it comes to a rolling boil, a spoon of baking soda is put in, which causes a violent rolling, mixing action. For this reason, the pot should not be over one-third full of water.

In the dry method, the furs to be blended are put in an electric blender, and will blend in about five seconds. As far as I know, Dave Engerbretson originally publicized this method and he has a full description of it in a piece in *Fly Fisherman* magazine for March 1971. He credits Jake Discher of the St. Paul Fly Tyers Club with originating the method.

I make many very large nymphs (Nos. 4, 3, and 4X long) and these require so much dubbing, which is difficult to apply, that I usually use a very fuzzy wool, angora, and acrylic blended yarn for bodies on these flies.

I have never had much success spinning fur on waxed thread for large flies, no matter how sticky the wax. About three years ago, a fellow named Jim Mitchell solved this problem for me. Jim uses a mixture of alcohol and stick shellac of about the consistency of thick syrup, which he paints on the tying thread with a toothpick. The fur adheres instantly, and the finished fly is extremely durable. It is the only method I use for fur now, but I still find the proper color and style of fuzzy yarns easier to use and if the fish can tell the difference, they haven't mentioned it to me.

Here are the patterns. Those with an asterisk are my own developments; the others are commercial patterns, taken from fly-sellers' catalogs and instruction books.

Skunk Hair Caddis

Little Green Caddis Pupa

Natant Nylon Nymph

Green Damsel Nymph

Assam Dragon

Group I Nymphs—Quill Gordon, Genie May, Zug Bug

Group II Nymphs—Sowbug, Grass Shrimp, Otter Shrimp

Hendrickson Nymph

Grey Nymph

ASSAM DRAGON*   (impressionistic, to represent any of several large genera of drag-
    onfly nymphs).

    Sizes: 4, 2X long, to 10, 3X long.

    Tail: None.

  Weight: Lead wire sized to hook size, 12 wraps.

    Body: Natural brown seal fur *on the skin*. A strip one-eighth inch wide for
           size 4 and one-sixteenth inch wide for smaller hooks is used. Should
           be 3 to 4 inches long.

  Hackle: Brown dyed grizzly, long and soft. I use cock capercaillie rump and
           flank feathers for my own, from a supply given me years ago. This
           bird is on the endangered list and its feathers not now available.

  Thread: 3/0 brown Nymo or similar. Wrap on the 12 turns of proper size
           lead wire, centering on the hook shank. Start the tying thread just
           back of the eye and spiral tightly back over the wire to the bend.
           Coat with lacquer. Cut the seal fur strip to a point on one end, tie
           this point on at the bend, tightly. Wind tying thread to eye. Wind
           the strip forward, each wrap just touching the one preceding. Stroke
           the fur toward the hook bend after each wrap. Tie off neatly. Take
           several more turns of tying thread at this point. Put on a drop of
           lacquer or cement. Tie the hackle in by the butt, with the wrong
           side toward the eye of the hook. This is just opposite of regular
           procedure. Wind one and one-half turns, tie off, clip off remainder
           of hackle, and finish the fly head. Soak the head well with cement
           or lacquer. This is a rough and scraggly looking fly, but so is the
           natural. It is an excellent nymph for larger trout.

Assam Dragon

BEAVERPELT   (impressionistic, this fly also represents dragonfly nymphs). Sizes 2
     through 8, 2X long.

Beaverpelt

   Tail: None.
  Body: Beaver fur, dubbed thicker toward head.
Thread: Brown Nymo 3/10.
Hackle: Long, soft natural black or Chinese pheasant green-black rump
           feather. Wrap hook with the desired size lead wire, 12 wraps,
           centered on shank. Spin on and dub beaver fur, making a thick,
           rough body, thicker toward head. Tie off one-eighth inch back of
           hook eye. Tie in hackle by butt, take two turns, tie off. Clip off
           excess hackle and finish head. Cement well.

BROWN STONE   (imitative of several medium-sized stonefly nymphs). Sizes 6
     through 10, 3X long.

       Tail: Several fibers of cock pheasant tail feather.
      Body: Gray, brown, tan, or black fur.
       Rib: Brown or orange buttonhole twist.
Wing cases: Section of cock pheasant tail feather.
    Hackle: Grouse body feather, color to suit body of fly.
    Thread: Size and color to match size and color of fly. Weight as desired.
               Start thread near bend, apply drop of cement, tie on several fibers
               for tail, long enough to show mottling. Tie in rib material. Spin fur
               on thread and wind on body, making thicker at thorax by winding
               back to base of same. Wind rib forward and tie off here. Tie in
               section of pheasant tail fibers of proper width for wing case, leaving
               one-third of feather to rear of tie-in point, butt of feather toward
               eye. Spiral thread forward, tie in and wind one turn grouse feather
               hackle. Tie off. Pull wing-case section forward down over back of
               thorax, folding hackle down under hook. Tie off just back of eye,
               clip off excess wing case at both ends. Finish head and lacquer or
               cement.

Brown Stone

CATSKILL COILER   (imitative of stoneflies of medium to large sizes). Sizes 6 to 10,
    3X long.

Tail:	Two hairs from peccary neck.
Body:	Brown, gray, black, or tan yarn.
Rib:	Brown or orange flat monofilament.
Legs:	Mottled grouse body feather.
Wing cases:	Darker grouse body feathers (2).
Collar:	Black, gray, or tan ostrich herl.
Thread:	Black or brown Nymo. To me, this is an unnecessarily complicated manner of making an imitative artificial: it is included here because some believe such close imitations are justified. You must first prepare the wings and legs of this fly before doing any of the other steps. The legs are prepared by stroking the chosen feather the wrong way. Then separate the legs, of about six or eight fibers each, with a dubbing needle. Put a drop of spar varnish at the base of each leg segment with the dubbing needle. Stroke each leg segment with a dubbing needle. Stroke each leg segment lightly toward the tip of its fibers with the fingers, forming the legs. Lay aside to dry. Prepare the wing cases by coating the underside of each with two or three coats of lacquer or head cement. Set aside to dry. Weight the hook with 12 to 15 wraps of the proper size wire, centered on shank. Tie on thread near eye, spiral back to bend. Coat entire shank and lead wire with cement. Tie the two peccary (javelina) hairs on at the bend, separated. Spiral thread to one-eighth inch back of eye. Tie in yarn, wind to bend, forward to eye, back to base of thorax, winding closely or more widely spaced as needed to give proper body shape. Tie off, wind rib material, tie off, clip thread. Put a large drop of some good adhesive on top of thorax. Rubber cement works well. Press legs down on this with feather stem extending out over eye of hook. When legs are dry, place a drop of cement on underside of each wing case (after trimmed to shape). Press down on top of legs, stems of feathers extending over eye of hook. The top wing case should be somewhat forward of the bottom wing case to give a natural appearance. When the wings have set, tie the stem ends down firmly, trim off excess. Tie in and wind ostrich herl collar. Tie off, clip excess. Finish and lacquer head.

Catskill Coiler

CREAM CADDIS   (imitative, though I know of no caddis of this size or color that
        does not make a case. The Cream Caddis represents an uncased larva).
        Sizes 8 to 14.

Tail:	None.
Body:	Creamy tan fur or yarn.
Rib:	Fine copper wire or buttonhole twist of brown or olive.
Thorax:	Gray or black ostrich herl.
Hackle:	Soft, short black.
Thread:	Tan Nymo 5/0. Weight as desired. Tie on thread at bend, tie in ribbing material. Spin on fur or tie in yarn and wind body for two-thirds of hook shank. Tie off, wind ribbing, and tie off. Tie in herl and wind thorax, full and thick, to one-eighth inch back of eye. Clip excess, tie in, and wind one turn of hackle. Tie off, clip excess, finish and lacquer head.

Cream Caddis

GREEN DAMSEL   (imitative of damselfly nymphs. The body color can be tan, olive,
        or gray also).

Sizes:	6 through 10, 3X long.
Tail:	Three strands of peacock sword (use ostrich herl for other colors).
Body:	Green fur or yarn.
Rib:	Gold oval tinsel.
Hackle:	Grizzly dyed green. Use hackles of other colors to match different colored bodies.
Thread:	Black or olive Nymo 3/0. Weight body with 15 turns of proper size wire. Tie in thread at eye and wind to bend. Lacquer entire shank. Tie in the tails; length should be half the body length. Tie in tinsel. Tie in yarn or fur at eye, wind to bend, forward to eye, back to base of thorax. Tie off. Wind rib to base of thorax, tie off. Tie in hackle by butt. Strip fibers off lower side of hackle. Wind two separated turns, one at base of thorax, one halfway between it and hook eye. Tie off, clip excess, wind thread forward, finish and lacquer head.

Green Damsel

GREY NYMPH   (suggestive, but one of the deadliest all-around nymph patterns). Sizes 6 through 14, 1X long.

   Tail: Badger hair.
   Body: Neutral gray fur; muskrat or similar.
Hackle: Soft gray grizzly.
Thread: Black Nymo. Weight as desired. Tie thread on at eye, wind to bend. Lacquer shank. Tie in tails, as long as body, a rather full tail. Tie off, spin on fur for a good thick body, somewhat thicker at front. Tie off one-eighth inch back of eye. Tie in and wind one and one-half turns of hackle. Clip excess; wind and finish head. A very simple but effective fly.

Grey Nymph

HARE'S EAR NYMPH   (suggestive, but very deadly when caddises are hatching, and effective almost any time. One of the best all-around nymph types). Sizes 8 through 14, 1X long.

      Tail: None or brown hackle fibers.
       Rib: Oval gold tinsel.
      Body: Fur from the face and head of a cottontail rabbit. Fur from the rest of the body is generally too long and dark. The finished fly should be more reddish brown than gray.
Wing cases: Mallard primary sections.
    Thread: Brown Nymo 5/0. Weight as desired. Tie in thread at front and wind to rear. Lacquer entire shank. Tie in ribbing. Spin fur on thread, wind to just back of eye. Body should taper only slightly. Tie off, wind rib, and tie off. Tie in wing sections just back of eye. Clip off excess, then clip off wing cases just above body level. Finish and lacquer head. The body and rib on this fly run the full length of the hook shank.

Gold Ribbed Hare's Ear

HENDRICKSON   (imitative of *Ephemerella subvaria*). Sizes 10 and 12, 1X long.

        Tail: Wood-duck flank fibers.
        Rib: Gold wire or orange thread.
       Body: Two-thirds muskrat fur, one-third brown seal fur, blended.
Wing cases: Blue gray wing fibers.
     Hackle: Grouse body feather.
     Thread: Olive Nymo 5/0. Weight as desired. Tie thread on at front, wind to
                bend. Lacquer entire shank. Tie in tails. Tie in ribbing, spin fur on
                thread and wind the body, tapering to a full thorax. Wind tying
                thread from just back of eye to rear of thorax. Wind ribbing and tie
                off. Tie in wing-case material, butt of fibers forward, with about
                one-third of the wing-case section to the rear. Wind thread forward
                to back of eye, tie in, and wind hackle. Pull wing-case material
                forward over thorax, tie down. Clip excess material off front and
                rear of wing case, wind and finish head.

Hendrickson

IDA MAY*   (designed to imitate *Ephemerella grandis* mayfly). Sizes 8 and 10, 1X
            long.

     Tail: Grizzly fibers dyed dark green.
      Rib: Peacock herl and gold wire.
     Body: Black fuzzy yarn or fur.
   Hackle: Grizzly dyed dark green.
   Thread: Black Nymo 5/0. Weight as desired. Tie in thread at eye, wind
              back to bend. Lacquer shank. Tie in tails, as long as body. Tie in
              herl and gold wire. Tie in body material, wind to eye and back to
              base of thorax. Tie off, clip excess. Wind peacock herl as rib, in
              normal manner. Tie off. Wind gold wire in opposite direction,
              pulling tightly so that it sinks out of sight in body material. Spiral

thread to front of body, tie in and wind one and one-half turns of hackle, which should be long and soft, to slant back over body. Finish and lacquer head.

Ida May

LITTLE GREEN CADDIS*   (imitative of pupal stage of *Rhyacophila* genus of caddis flies). Sizes 12 to 16, 1X long.

Tail:	None.
Egg sac:	Tuft of fluorescent green yarn.
Body:	Hunter's green yarn.
Rib:	Gold wire.
Thorax:	Tan or gray ostrich herl, two strands.
Wings:	Ends of above.
Hackle:	Grouse body feather.

Little Green Caddis

Thread: Olive Nymo 6/0. Weight as desired, using fine lead wire, as the body of this fly must not be too thick. Tie in thread at eye and wind to bend. Lacquer shank. Tie in tuft of brightest green wool possible to find. Clip short and fuzz out to make egg sac. Tie in gold wire and yarn. Wind yarn to make a body the same size from bend to thorax. Tie off, wind rib. Tie off, tie in ostrich herl, wind both strands to make thorax. Tie off just back of eye, clip ends so they are same length as hook shank. Tie in and wind one turn of hackle. Tie off, finish and lacquer head.

LITTLE GREY CADDIS*   (imitates *Brachycentrus* genus of caddis flies). Sizes 12 to 18, 1X long. This fly is tied exactly as is the Little Green Caddis except that the body is dark gray yarn. There are no other changes.

Little Grey Caddis

MARCH BROWN   (imitative, although exactly what it imitates is a matter of disagreement. It will work for both mayfly and stonefly nymphs, and is a very good pattern for most waters. The original was British, and different British writers applied the name to different species, some to a mayfly that hatched in March, others to a stonefly that hatched in the same month. Skues regarded it as a brown sedge (caddis). In the United States, both Art Flick (*Streamside Guide*) and Preston Jennings (*A Book of Trout Flies*) regard it as imitating *Stenonema vicarium* of the mayfly group and call it the American March Brown). Sizes 8 through 14, 1X long.

Tail:	Fibers of cock pheasant tail.
Body:	Blend of one-third gray muskrat and two-thirds brown seal.
Rib:	Light brown buttonhole twist.
Wing cases:	Section of fibers of cock pheasant tail.
Hackle:	Grouse body feather, brown rather than gray.
Thread:	Tan Nymo 5/0. Weight as desired. Tie in thread at front, wind to bend. Lacquer shank. Tie in tails, as long as the body. Spin on fur and wind body tapering and full at the thorax. Finish with thread at base of thorax. Wind rib and tie off. Tie section of wing-case material at base of thorax, one-third of section extending to rear, butts of section toward eye. Wind thread forward, tie in and wind one turn of hackle. Pull wing-case butt section forward and tie down, forcing hackles to side and below hook. Clip excess, front and back, wind and finish head.

March Brown

MARTINEZ BLACK   (impressionistic of dark mayfly and stonefly nymphs of medium size). Sizes 8 through 14, 1X long.

       Tail: Guinea spotted flank feather fibers.

       Rib: Fine copper wire.

    Body: Black seal fur.

  Thorax: Black chenille.

Wing cases: The original calls for bright green raffia. I have had better success with dyed green primary sections.

  Hackle: Soft grizzly (hen neck hackle works great).

  Thread: Black Nymo 5/0. Weight as desired. Tie in thread at front and wind to bend. Lacquer shank. Tie in tail fibers as long as body. Tie in rib. Spin on fur and wind to base of thorax. Tie off, wind ribbing, and tie off. Tie in black chenille of a size so that one turn will make a full thorax. Tie in wing-case section with tips toward bend. Wind thread forward, wind one turn of chenille, tie off. Pull wing-case section forward on top of thorax and tie down at front. Clip excess, leaving a short stub protruding at rear of thorax. Tie in and wind one turn of hackle. Tie off, clip excess, finish head.

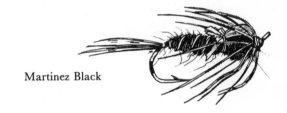

Martinez Black

MONTANA STONE*   (imitates *Pteronarcys* genus of stoneflies, especially *P. californica*). Sizes 4, 4X long, to 8, 3X long. Weight as desired. I weight the No. 4, 4X long model with 25 turns of .030-inch lead wire.

       Tail: Six fibers of raven or crow primary.

       Rib: Copper wire.

    Body: Black fuzzy yarn, four strand.

  Hackle: One grizzly saddle and one grizzly dyed dark brown. Strip hackles off lower side of each hackle before tying in.

Gills: Light gray or white ostrich herl.

Thread: Black Nymo 3/0. Tie in thread at front, wind to bend. Lacquer shank. Tie in tail fibers and split to form forked tail, three fibers per side. Tie in ribbing and yarn. Wind thread forward, half hitch twice, and break off. Lacquer shank again. Wind yarn to eye, back to bend, forward to eye, and back to base of thorax. Tie off, tying in thread at same time. Wind rib and tie off. Tie in one strand of ostrich herl, and both hackles by the butts. Strip fibers off lower side of both hackles. Wind two separated turns of hackle, one at the base of the thorax and one halfway between there and the eye. Both colors of hackle should lie one against the other. Tie off. Wind ostrich herl forward at the base of the hackles, tie off. Spiral thread forward and finish head large and lacquer well.

Montana Stone

OTTER SHRIMP   (suggestive of any of the various scuds such as *Gammarus* and *Hyalella*, and perhaps others. The original was developed by Ted True-blood).

Tail: Grouse body feather fibers.

Body: Grayish otter fur with a smidgin of brown seal mixed in. How much is a smidgin? Don't ask.

Hackle: Grouse body feather.

Thread: Olive Nymo 6/0. Weight as desired, using fine wire. Tie on thread at front, wind to bend. Lacquer shank. Tie in tails, short. Spin on fur and wind to just back of eye, making body taper to full front section. Tie in a few hackles, bearded underneath. Finish and lacquer head. A very effective fly in lakes, ponds, and weedy streams.

Otter Shrimp

QUILL GORDON   (imitates *Eporus (Iron) fraudator* mayfly). Sizes 12 and 14, 1X long.

Tail: Wood-duck flank fibers.

Body: Tannish gray muskrat fur, more gray than tan.

Wing cases: Dark Mallard flank feather.

Hackle: Soft ginger.

Thread: Olive Nymo 6/0. Weight with a very fine wire. Tie in thread at front, wind to rear. Lacquer shank. Tie in tails, as long as body. Spin fur on thread and wind body, tapering to full thorax. Finish just back of eye. Tie in and wind one turn of hackle. Tie on section of mallard so that it lies on top of thorax, extending one-third of way to bend. Pull hackle down and to side. Clip excess. Finish and lacquer head.

Quill Gordon

SHRIMP   (suggests any of the shrimp-scud family). Sizes 8 through 16.

Tail: None.

Rib: Orange, brown, or olive buttonhole twist.

Body: Two separate colors of yarn put on in two different manners. Yarns in the pattern described here are small pale green and larger light gray.

Hackle: Pale ginger.

Thread: Tan Nymo 6/0. Weight as desired, using fine wire. Tie in thread at front, wind to bend. Lacquer shank. Tie in ribbing and green yarn. Wind thread to front. Wind green yarn to just back of eye, tie off. Spiral thread to bend, tie in, and palmer hackle *and thread* to just back of eye. Tie off, make two half hitches, clip thread, and seal with a drop of lacquer or cement. Retie thread in at bend. Trim hackle off top of shank. Tie in four strands of yarn about twice the diameter of the green yarn at the bend. Half hitch twice, break thread, seal with a drop of cement. Retie thread just back of eye.

Pull the four strands of gray yarn forward, two on top, one on each side of the hook. Pull quite tight, tie off, clip excess. Wind ribbing forward over everything, weaving through the hackles underneath so as not to bind them down. Tie off ribbing, clip excess. Finish and lacquer head.

Grass Shrimp

SKUNK HAIR CADDIS*   (imitates larger cased caddis such as *Hesperophylax* or other genera that make case of small stones and grains of sand). Sizes 6 through 10, 2X long.

Tail: None.

Body: Black or blackish brown skunk tail hair, with the black portion at least 4 inches long.

Rib: Copper wire.

Hackle: Black, short, and soft.

Thread: Black Nymo 2/0. Weight hook as desired, centering wire on the shank. Tie in thread at the eye, wind tightly to bend. Lacquer shank. Tie in a good bunch of hair about the size of a kitchen match. Tie in hair by the tips *after* the tips have been evened up. Lash hair down *very* firmly. Wind thread to just back of eye. Twist hair counterclockwise and commence to wind on in tight turns. Twist hair more after each turn is completed. Tie down just back of eye *very* tightly. Clip off excess hair carefully. Take a few more winds over hair butts, soak with lacquer or cement. Tie in rib, wind to bend and back, tie off. Clip excess. Tie in hackle and wind one turn. Tie off, clip excess, and finish head very large. Lacquer well. This is a difficult fly to make, due to the difficulty of tying the hair down so that it will not loosen, and to keeping it twisted tightly enough so that the turns remain separate. It is the best cased caddis imitation I know of, and has taken many fish for me over twenty some years. I just wish that there was an easier way to tie it.

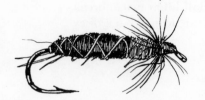

Skunk Hair Caddis

SOW BUG   (suggests aquatic sow bugs, and possibly the smaller scuds). Sizes 14
through 18, 1X long.

     Tail: Piece of light gray or whitish soft wing primary section.

   Body: Tan, light gray, or cream fur or yarn.

    Rib: Olive or dark brown buttonhole twist.

Thread: Olive Nymo 6/0. Weight as desired with finest lead wire centered
on shank. Tie in thread at eye, wind to bend. Lacquer shank. Tie in
narrow piece of primary section at bend with short section of the tip
protruding rearward. Divide this section to make forked tail.
Lacquer tails *and* remainder of primary section. Tie in ribbing, and
body material. Wind body material to eye, making body fuller in
center, tapered to each end. Tie off, clip excess. Bring rest of
primary section forward over back, pull tight, and tie off at eye.
Clip excess. Wind rib forward tightly to eye, tie off, clip excess.
Finish head small, lacquer head and back.

Sow Bug

WOOLY WORM   (suggestive of many kinds of underwater creatures—stoneflies,
dragonflies, riffle beetle larvae, hellgrammites, damselflies, and who knows
what. Doubt if it is ever taken for a caterpillar). Sizes 4, 4X long, through
10, 3X long.

    Tail   None.

   Body: Chenille of proper size and color to suit. Black, olive green, brown,
and yellow seem most productive.

Hackle: Grizzly is first and original choice, but brown, black, ginger, and
badger are all used. Weight as desired. Tie in thread (black, and of
a size to suit the hook size) at eye and wind to bend. Lacquer
shank. Tie in chenille, and proper size hackle, by the tip. Wind
body to eye and tie off. Wind hackle to eye, tie off. Finish head
large and lacquer well. Seven turns of hackle is the accepted

standard, but I prefer five turns for a somewhat sparser fly. The original of this fly did not have tails or ribbing and that is the way I have always used them.

Wooly Worm

YELLOW STONE* (imitates *Acroneuria* genus of stoneflies and will work well for *Perla* also). Sizes 4, 3X long, through 10, 3X long.

Tail:	Cinnamon turkey primary fibers, six to eight fibers.
Body:	Mottled brown yarn with a yellowish cast.
Rib:	Antique gold yarn and gold wire.
Hackle:	One grizzly saddle and one grizzly dyed brown.
Gills:	Light gray or white ostrich herl.
Thread:	Tan Nymo 3/0 to 5/0. Weight as desired. Tie in thread at eye, wind to bend. Lacquer shank. Tie in tail fibers, long; divide evenly for forked tail. Tie in gold wire. Tie in yarn at eye, wind to bend, forward to near eye, back to base of thorax. Tie off. Tie in one strand of four-strand gold antique yarn. Wind this as rib to bend and back to base of thorax, X fashion. Tie off, clip excess. Wind gold wire tightly forward to base of thorax, tie off, and clip excess. If this wire is not pulled very tight, the X ribbing will slip to the bend of the hook during casting. Tie in both hackles by butts after stripping lower side of hackles. Tie in ostrich herl. Wind hackles two separate turns, one at base of thorax, one halfway between there and eye. Both color hackles must be together. Tie off, clip excess. Wind herl forward at base of hackles. Tie off, clip excess. Wind thread forward, finish head large. Lacquer well. If you cannot find a blended yarn that looks mottled, use brown melody yarn, which can be found at most large yarn shops.

Yellow Stone

ZUG BUG   (whether this fly is suggestive or impressionistic is open to question. Whatever, it is one of the more effective general nymph types wherever dark nymphs exist). Sizes 4, 2X long, to 14, 2X long.

Tail:	Three strands of sword peacock, long.
Body:	Peacock herl, full.
Rib:	Oval silver tinsel.
Wing case:	Mallard flank.
Hackle:	Soft brown.
Thread:	Olive Nymo 5/0. Weight as desired. Tie in thread at eye, wind to bend. Lacquer shank. Tie in tails, as long as hook shank. Clip excess, tie in rib and body material. Wind thread forward to just back of eye. Wind body full, to just back of eye. Tie off, clip excess. Wind rib three turns to front of body, tie off. Clip excess, tie in mallard flank on top, as wing case. Tie in hackle, wind one turn, tie off. Clip excess, finish and lacquer head.

Zug Bug

Almost none of these patterns, except the Catskill Coiler, are completely standardized; thus the materials and instructions given here are a compromise. In most cases, I have tried to use materials that are readily available; but for the past few years, I have been unable to find a fly materials shop anywhere that carried a really complete selection, and even with what I could find in hobby, sewing, and yarn shops, I have had to buy from several houses to get a more complete selection of the materials I needed. Even then, some things could not be found. I have ordered skunk tails from five different material houses in the past eighteen months, in an effort to get tails that had hair that had black tips at least four inches long. None of the tails I received had hair with black tips over two and a half inches long, and so were not usable for the purpose for which I wanted them. At present, I am searching for a substitute for skunk tail hair for making my Skunk Hair Caddis.

Also, these houses were unable to furnish natural brown seal fur on the skin. This material can be found in shops and factories that make fur coats, as scraps and trimmings, as can other kinds of fur trimmings very useful to the flytier. For the last four years I have had to depend on friends who lived in cities that had fur coat manufacturers to supply me with natural brown seal fur. If you live in a place that might have someone who makes fur coats, look them up in the phone book and call on them in person. Your eyes will probably bulge out at the fine supply of fur and hair scraps they will sell you for a pittance.

Below is a list of fly material houses that I have dealt with over the years. Some will carry products that others will not and I have found it necessary to have at all times several sources, and as mentioned earlier, even then some things could not be obtained.

DAN BAILEY'S FLY SHOP
209 West Park Street
Livingston, Montana 59047

PAT BARNES
West Yellowstone, Montana 59758

BODMER'S FLY SHOP
2400 Naegele Road
Colorado Springs, Colorado 80904

BUZ'S FLY AND TACKLE SHOP
805 West Tulare Avenue
Visalia, California 93277

FIRESIDE ANGLER
P. O. Box 823
Melville, New York 11746

HARRY A. DARBEE
Livingston Manor, New York 12758

HERTER'S, INC.
Route 2
Mitchell, South Dakota 57301

E. HILLE
P. O. Box 269
Williamsport, Pennsylvania 17701

BOB JACKLIN'S FLY SHOP
P. O. Box 604
West Yellowstone, Montana 59758

KAUFMANN'S STREAMBORN FLIES
P. O. Box 23032
13055 S. W. Pacific Highway
Portland, Oregon 97223

BUD LILLY'S TROUT SHOP
P. O. Box 387
West Yellowstone, Montana 59758

FLY FISHERMAN'S BOOKCASE
3890 Stewart Road
Eugene, Oregon 97402

Bud Lilly's shop, with which I was associated for some years, has taken the trouble to obtain materials for my patterns of nymphs that use materials not found in most shops. However, even this shop has been unable to find skunk tails of the proper kind. Also, natural seal fur on the skin, in strips of four inches long or longer, is not usually available at this or most other shops. Bud issues the finest tackle catalog that I know of, not excepting Orvis or Dan Bailey.

Pat Barnes carries some models of the Sealey hooks that I prefer; he has a good selection of the larger sizes of nymph hooks. His wife, Sig, is one of the best flytiers in the country.

Bob Jacklin carries some items not generally found in other shops, including a really good copper ribbing wire, and some specialty items. He is one of the best flytiers around also and puts out a good catalog.

George Bodmer is a prime source of flies that are not only excellent but many of which are not available elsewhere. This includes the Colorado King, the best dry caddis pattern I have ever used, with the possible exception of Al Troth's Elk Hair Caddis, which is equally good. However, the Colorado King is available in more colors and sizes.

Herter's used to have more fly-tying items than any other house, but since they have expanded into many other fields, they have slipped in the fly materials department. Herter's carries Sealey hooks, but I must advise that the Sealey firm has changed hands and that quality control is nowhere near as good as it was. For this reason I have switched to using the Partridge hooks available from Angler's Mail, 6497 Pearl Road, Cleveland, Ohio 44130.

The Streamborn Flies Catalog has by far the largest selection of nymph patterns of any catalog I know of, and many of the patterns are very good. The large stone and dragon fly nymphs they sell are the best commercial versions I have seen. Randall Kaufmann, in July 1975, published the *American Nymph Fly Tying Manual*. This is a very good manual and pictures and descriptions are clear. Part III, Nymph Pattern Dictionary, lists 200 patterns (including those in the tying section). As is generally true throughout the world of fly-tying and nymph fishing, most of the patterns are nonspecific. It is not the fault of the author; it is just the way things are.

The following are shops I know only through friends who have dealt with them and found them satisfactory.

ANGLER'S ROOST	LEN CODELLA
141 East 44th Street	Angler's Den
New York, New York 10017	5 South Wood Avenue
	Linden, New Jersey 07037

There are several good recent books on fly-tying for the beginner. For the experienced flytier who is interested in nymphs, and perhaps some special methods, I recommend the three books below:

Tying and Fishing the Fuzzy Nymphs by E. H. Polly Rosborough (Manchester, Vermont: The Orvis Co., 1969).

Art Flick's Master Fly-Tying Guide (New York: Crown Publishers, 1972).

Fly-Tying Materials by Eric Leiser (New York: Crown Publishers, 1973).

Polly Rosborough's book is very good overall, and even his suggestive nymph patterns are excellent.

Art Flick's *Guide* contains a series of methods of tying a wide selection of different kinds of flies by nationally known experts.

Leiser's work is the most thorough and complete on the subject of fly-tying materials that I have met with and every serious flytier will find much of value in it. I dislike the emphasis on Mustad hooks, but Leiser and others who are in the retail hook business apparently feel that these hooks are adequate, and that their availability is a necessary factor. Personally, I would use them *only* if I could not get *any* brand of British hooks. I once had to buy a huge quantity of them to fill some fly orders, but the orders fell through and I later discarded the Mustad hooks, nearly ten thousand of them. I feel that they simply are not fly quality hooks in spite of the millions of them being used for that purpose.

In the use of hooks, I am adamant. A good fly requires a good deal of time and materials and I feel it just isn't good common sense not to use the best hooks available. The price of the very best British hooks is no more than similar sizes of other types of so-called fly hooks, and is a tiny fraction of the cost of the fly. Flies selling for seventy-five cents apiece can be tied on the best of British hooks at a cost of less than two cents per hook.

Other materials I do not feel so strongly about. No fly dressing is sacred, as has been proven over the years by the tampering with patterns, even old and good patterns, which is evident in even the best fly-tying shops.

Roy Steenrod has complained bitterly over the years that no one ties his fine dry fly, the Hendrickson, true to pattern. Elizabeth Grieg, perhaps the most famous woman flytier, stated over thirty years ago that none of the fly shops carried flies that were tied true to pattern. But the tampering with patterns did not start on this side of the Atlantic. In *A History of Fly Fishing for Trout*, John Waller Hills traces many patterns over a period of four or five hundred years, during which time materials and even color and form changed. As long ago as that, flytiers were seeking ways to tie a more representative pattern, or introducing different, and what some thought were better, materials.

As I said earlier, it is the final result that counts, and this, along with the fact that everyone sees that result differently, makes a complete, formal standard of any pattern unlikely, if not impossible.

So, if you are a flytier as well as a fly-fisher, by all means tie the fly the way *you* want it. Exact imitation is never possible, and confidence in the fly being used is a more important factor anyway. I don't really believe in imitation, though I use the word as a convenience; "simulation" would be a better term.

In small nymphs, which are mostly used in smooth water, color, form, and size should be as close as possible to that of the natural. Very large nymphs, 4s and 6s, which are generally used in rough, fast water, work better, in my experience, if they give a general, somewhat blurred impression of the natural. I try to represent only the salient features of such big nymphs. I have experimented with them for over fifteen years, and have come to the conclusion that nymphs without wing cases work as well as those with wing cases, and work even better in very rough water. The reason is that such turbulent water turns and twists the line and leader, and thus the fly. All my fast-water nymphs are tied in "the round," that is, so that all sides look alike. Thus, since the fly has no top, bottom, or sides, it always looks right side up, no matter what turning and twisting the line and leader do. Also, I feel that this type of tie makes it very difficult for the fish to detect unnatural motion.

During the time I was becoming a nymph fisherman, I spent a total of about thirteen hours underwater in trout-holding water studying the actions of natural

Some basic reference books

and artificial nymphs, and the reaction of the trout to them. I don't recommend this for the average nymph fisherman, but you should be thinking about what is going on down there, and when you sit down to your vise, or walk into a fly shop, you should have in mind the actions and habitat of the artificial you are tying or selecting. If you don't, you are wasting your time and money.

One of the factors always to be considered is size. Nymphs grow throughout their underwater life, and if the nymph you are simulating in your fishing in April hatches into the adult in June, then you must use an artificial that matches its April, not its June, size. If it hatches as a size 10, it will be no larger than a size 12 or 14 in April.

One other thing to remember, which has been completely ignored throughout fly-fishing history, is that nymphs are no different in their growth patterns than are other creatures, and nymphs of the same age and species in the same stretch of water will vary in size just as children in the same grade in school will. There will always be a variance of sizes in the same species in the same water any time. It may be that the size representing the largest of those present will take more or larger fish, but a smaller size of the same pattern will also probably work, and sometimes a slightly oversized pattern will work best of all. Therefore, I like to have three sizes of patterns of each species. I use the smaller size earlier in the year, the middle size in the month before the nymph is due to hatch into the adult form, and the largest size in the last few days prior to the expected hatch.

It is sometimes possible to work backward from a result in nymph fishing to identify a natural of which the artificial came first. It has happened to me twice, both times because of accidents. Some time ago, I ordered some material from a fly-tying materials house. When it arrived, through a mistake, one skein of chenille that should have been black turned out to be a dark purple. At first I was tempted to send it back, but my brother and a sister and her husband live in Missouri and fish the Ozark streams for bass, and purple is one of the better bass fly body colors. So I decided to use up the purple material in making bass flies. I made up some purple bodied streamers on which my brother Ken hooked the largest bass of his life. I also made up a few big purple bodied nymphs with a burnt orange hackle. My brother-in-law, Red James, caught a six-and-one-half-pound brown on this nymph the first time he used it in one of the Yellowstone Park streams.

I was puzzled as to what this nymph could possibly imitate, but in searching through my insect books I found three nymphs that have a purplish cast to the body. The largest of these was the damselfly nymph, *Argia violocea;* another, almost as large, was the largest of the mayfly nymphs, *Hexagenia bilineata;* the third, a smaller mayfly nymph, *Isonychia velma.*

I found both the damselfly and the *Isonychia* mayfly nymphs in different sections of the stream where Red caught his lunker brown, and finding the *Hexagenia* in the book solved another problem that had been puzzling me. Several years before I had fished for grayling in Grebe Lake in the Park with Jim Begley and his son Dr. Lew Begley. Lew had outfished both of his elders with a large nymph with a dark purple body and a collar of soft black hackle.

After finding *Hexagenia bilineata* in the book, I went back to Grebe and found the natural in the soft silt near the outlet, the spot where Lew's artificial had been so effective. However, I am not sure the natural was *bilineata*, it may have been *recurvata;* its size more nearly matches the latter. Except for size, the two are similar in other respects, including habits and habitat.

I have refined the dressings and now use the three dressed as follows:

GENIE MAY*   (imitates *Hexagenia bilineata* or *recurvata*). Size 6, 2X long.

Tail:	Fibers of grizzly dyed dark orange.
Body:	Brown Mohlon.
Rib:	Strand of dark purple wool and gray ostrich herl.
Overrib:	Gold wire reverse wound.
Hackle:	Grizzly dyed dark orange.
Thread:	Brown Nymo. Weight as desired. Wind on lead wire centered on shank. Start tying thread just back of eye, wind over lead wire to bend. Lacquer shank. Tie on good clump of hackle fibers for tail. Tie *one* strand of purple wool, one gray ostrich herl, and piece of gold wire. Wind thread to eye, tie in brown Mohlon, wind to bend, forward to eye, back to base of thorax. Tie off, clip excess. Wind purple wool as rib to base of thorax, wind ostrich herl against purple wool, tie off, clip excess of both materials. Overwind gold wire opposite direction to wool and herl, pulling down into body material. Tie off, clip. Tie in one hackle by butt, fibers stripped off

lower side. Wind two separated turns, one at base of thorax, one halfway between there and eye. Tie off, clip, wind thread forward, finish and lacquer head.

MISS TAKE*   (imitates *Argia violocea* damselfly nymph). Size 6, 3X long.

Tails: Peacock sword.

Body: Mottled brown wool.

Rib: Purple wool and ostrich herl, gray.

Overrib: Gold wire.

Hackle: Brown dyed grizzly, two separated turns.

Thread: Brown Nymo. Weight as desired. Tie on thread at eye and overwind lead wire to bend. Lacquer shank. Tie on tails, using thread between each strand so that tails will remain separate. Tie on one strand of purple wool, ostrich herl, and gold wire. Take thread to eye, tie on body yarn, wind to bend, forward to eye, back to base of thorax. Tie off, clip excess. Wind purple rib, with ostrich herl close up against it. Tie off, clip excess. Overwind gold wire in the opposite direction, tie off, clip. Tie in hackle by butt, lower fibers stripped off. Wind two separated turns of hackle, one at base of thorax, one halfway between there and eye. Tie off, clip excess, wind thread forward, finish and lacquer head. The name refers to the fact that this nymph came about largely by accident.

Miss Take

VELMA MAY*   (imitates *Isonychia velma*). Size 10, 3X long.

Tail: Grizzly hackle fibers dyed dark green.

Body: Mottled brown wool.

Rib: Purple wool, one strand, and gray ostrich herl.

Overrib: Gold wire.

Hackle: Grizzly dyed dark green.

Thread: Olive Nymo. Weight as desired. Tie in thread at eye, wind over lead wire to bend. Lacquer shank. Tie on good bunch of fibers for tails. Tie on body material, one strand purple wool, ostrich herl, gold wire. Wind thread to eye. Wind body material to eye, back to base of thorax. Tie off, clip excess. Wind purple wool and herl for rib, one against the other. Tie off, clip. Overwind gold wire tightly in reverse direction. Tie off, clip. Tie in hackle by butt, lower fibers stripped off. Wind two separated turns, one at base of thorax, one halfway between there and eye. Tie off, clip, wind thread forward, finish and lacquer head.

Velma May

This fly works very well in stretches of the Madison and Firehole in Yellowstone Park, and Henry's Fork of the Snake, where the natural does not dwell. It is possible that it is taken for *Ephemerella grandis* (Ida May), or perhaps some other species I have not found yet. The purple rib on all three flies is made by taking one strand of four-strand yarn, twisting it to make firm as it is wound on.

The flies just described are recent developments of mine and perhaps are not as good representations of the natural as I can, and eventually will, make. Nearly all my artificials go through a steady change over a period of years, as I try to obtain a more effective pattern.

One such pattern is the most effective emergent I have ever found. It grew, over a period of five to seven years, from a floating Hare's Ear nymph through several stages into its present form. It is fussy to make and not overly durable, but is the most useful and valuable emergent I have, and its chief value lies in the fact that it represents several genera, even separate orders of naturals.

NATANT NYLON NYMPH*   (impressionistic). Sizes 8 through 18, 2X long.

Tail: Fibers of grouse or grizzly, sparse and short.
Body: Black, brown, gray, or tan wool.
Rib: Gold wire.
Wing: Composite, of a square of nylon stocking enclosing polypropylene of gray or light tan.

Hackle: Grouse or grizzly fibers, bearded.

Thread: 5/0 Nymo, brown or tan. This nymph is never weighted. Start tying thread just back of eye, wind to where base of thorax would be. Make the wing by taking a 3/4-by-1 1/2-inch piece of stocking material, folding it double to make it square. Use light color stocking with light bodies, dark stocking for dark bodies. The size piece given is for size 10. Use larger strips for larger flies, smaller for smaller flies. In the center of the stocking material place a little ball of tan or gray polypropylene body material. Fold the stocking material around the poly to make a pouch. Tie the base of the pouch on hook at the wing position so that a little lump of stocking-enclosed poly sits on top of the hook. Wind thread around base of pouch *above* the top of the shank to make pouch and contents sit upright. Trim excess stocking material. Coat pouch and base where tied to hook shank with two coats of lacquer. Wind thread to bend, tie on tails, body, and ribbing material. Wind thread to eye. Wind tapering body to just back of eye. Thorax will be formed by the yarn being wound over the wing base. Wind rib full length of body, tie off. Clip yarn and wire excess. Tie in small bunch of *short* hackle fibers, bearded. Finish and lacquer head.

Natant Nylon Nymph

The problem in making this fly is caused by getting the pouch of stocking material with its enclosed poly ball to sit upright on the hook *and* in trimming off the excess stocking material without clipping the tying thread. All other operations are fairly normal.

Floated in the surface film, perhaps by use of a little grease on the wing pouch, this can be used during preemergence of nearly all mayfly types, and will work in very cold weather and water conditions to represent hatching caddises that seem to get stuck near the surface under such conditions.

My theory is that the "wing" does not actually represent just the wing of the emerging natural, but represents the entire insect bulging up through the split nymphal shuck. I may be wrong, but I have had better success with this emergent type than any other.

For fishing ponds, lakes, deep slow pools, and backwaters, one needs a pattern that simulates midge, blackfly, mosquito, and other larvae. I use the same pattern and size in several streams, ponds, and lakes in this area, and feel a wide selection of this artificial is not necessary.

CREAM WIGGLER* (impressionistic). Sizes 18 through 22, 2X short, 2X fine. This fly has only a "body" and a very short sparse hackle. The body is a one-half-inch strip of a car-washing chamois (shammy), the thickness of a tooth-pick tied at the center of the shank by one end, the full length left hanging loose. One turn of very short, very soft watery-colored grouse hackle is made just in front of where the shammy is tied on. The head is finished somewhat large. Use brown or tan tying thread.

Cream Wiggler

I formerly made the "body" of this larvae imitation from cream rubber strips, but the shammy when wet is more realistic and gives better action. This fly should be fished so that it hangs head up in the surface film. Greasing the head and hackle but *not* the body will usually accomplish this. Sometimes it is necessary to grease all but the last foot of leader.

I think it is fairly obvious that it will be necessary to reevaluate your artificial nymphs and larvae continually, and to redesign them as you learn more about their use, and about the natural they represent. For this reason, the fly-fisher who is also a flytier has a great advantage over his brother angler who is not.

19 The Roundup

YOU CANNOT STEP INTO THE SAME RIVER TWICE, SAID HERACLITUS ABOUT TWENTY-five hundred years ago, and of course, it is still true. For that reason the nymph fisherman's work is never done. Because running water is constantly changing, renewing itself, carving away at banks and bed, because its volume and temperature change constantly, its insect structure is also constantly changing and one must continually check and recheck his favorite waters to be informed.

Some protest that so much work leaves them little time for fishing. I sympathize with these fellows, because for years I had the same feeling. But after one gets well acquainted with the insect structures in his favorite waters, an hour spent in checking twice or three times a year will enable the angler to keep up with current and long-term changes. Or perhaps one can find a buddy to help with the situation. But beware: be sure your buddy and you can talk the same language.

A few years back I delegated a young fellow to screen a piece of water for me and to let me know what he found. The lad was a biology major and had exhibited considerable interest in underwater insects and I had mistaken interest for knowledge. When we got together that evening, I queried him as to what insects he had found.

"Well," he said, "there were a lot of shiny black ones, quite a few dark green ones, and a whole bunch of wiggly gray ones."

I suppose I shouldn't have been surprised, but just then I felt as though I had loaned one of my rare fishing books to a comic book reader.

While we are speaking of books, it might be time to remind you that you will

177

need and use many books in your underwater research. It isn't always necessary or even desirable to buy such books. Use the libraries of nearby colleges and universities. They will generally allow residents of the state or city in which they are located full use of in-house facilities, and state and land-grant colleges will grant inter-library loan privileges; they can get books for you from other libraries that they themselves don't have.

You can find much valuable material in the unpublished master's theses and doctor's dissertations, and the bibliographies in these papers are gold mines; you will find out about many books and other sources that you have never heard of before.

Most of these papers will be of regional, not national interest. Also, they will tend to be investigations of waters not too far from the college or university that the student attended. For this reason these studies will most often be of value to the angler who fishes locally, although there are occasions when insect studies will have national interest.

An example of a local study of considerable importance to the nymph fisher is *A Comparative Study of the Aquatic Insect Populations of Rock Creek, Montana, and Its Major Tributaries* by Ralph E. Driear of the University of Montana at Missoula (1974).

This study describes the habitat and location of eighty-six species of insects, and included stream maps on which each species is located. The bibliography is extensive. I feel that not only is this study of great value to the local angler, it would be to the visitor also, if he was informed enough to search the university library for it or similar studies.

Insect *identification* studies of national importance have been done by graduate students at several universities recently but I really feel that these are not as valuable to the nymph fisherman as are those that tell him what insects will be found where in the streams he fishes. The Driear thesis is like having a map of buried treasure for one who fishes Rock Creek.

Library personnel are among the nicest and most obliging of people. They seem to feel an eagerness to help disperse the vast information at their disposal and will often go far out of their way to lend a helping hand. They all seem to have an abiding love of books and learning and establish instant rapport with anyone who comes earnestly seeking knowledge.

While you are making your studies of underwater insects (on stream), it is a good idea to keep looking at the stream for sources of danger to them. If the insects go, the fish are doomed, and a changing insect structure is often a forerunner of a ruined stream. Insects have been on earth—in streams—for over two hundred million years. Some genera and species have been wiped out by the activities of man in less than a hundred years.

I have met up with fishermen who have replaced continued learning with constant refining of technique. They have achieved results that have led them into believing that they are learning new things. It is good to refine one's technique but there is a limit. Only so much gold will be found in a yard of gravel, and putting it through a sieve a thousand times will not increase the amount of gold by so much as a grain.

Studying insects in connection with trout fishing is like living in a house with a million rooms. Opening a door to any of these only reveals the contents of that room—and some more doors. But as long as one is not overcome by the enormity of the task and proceeds one room at a time, a lifetime of joyous learning lies ahead.

One of the things you will learn somewhere down the line is that it is insect activity that begets fish activity. There are times when underwater insects become so active that the stream bed is alive with moving insects. It starts with one or more species beginning to feed (the insects, not the fish) and this causes insect predators to start moving, seeking out their prey. Other insects commence to flee the predators, and a whole chain reaction is set in motion, ending with the fish feeding furiously.

When this activity commences, the trout will feed indiscriminately, but as it progresses, they will settle down to taking one species; that which is most numerous, largest, or easiest captured. If you are fishing when such a period starts, the trout will take about any nymph, yours included. But after the period is well established, you will need the right imitation fished in the right manner or you may find your artificial entirely ignored even though fish are feeding all around you. At these times the fish are hyperselective.

At other times, if the fish are hungry, just the opposite will occur. The fish will snap up any nymph he can find and your artificial as well. It is such times as these that bring about the apparent paradox of several fishermen fishing the same stretch at the same time, all with different flies and all catching fish.

Another reason for such a condition may rest with the preferences of the fish themselves. Fish are individuals, in behavior as well as appetite, and if several kinds of food are available for the gathering, one fish may prefer tiny insects that are inactive and plentiful to larger ones that are scarcer and more active. I had a perfect example of such preferment come to my attention last fall.

I had been out of the hospital only a while; the doctor forbade any fishing for at least six months and I got my information due to the concern of some friends. Koke Winter had called to say that he, Bob Jacklin, and Jim Vermillion were going to fish the Madison estuary that evening and wanted to know if I would like a fish or two, since they knew my penchant for examining stomach contents regularly. I replied in the affirmative also giving them the word from my ninety-two-year-old mother-in-law that she would welcome a fish for the table.

Koke brought the fish in late in the evening, the last two the fellows had caught before quitting, a brown and a rainbow of eighteen inches, almost identical in size and weight. One had been caught on a wet fly, one on a large Spruce streamer.

The stomach contents were startling. Both had been caught within a long cast of each other over a silt bottom, and both were gorged. The stomach of the brown contained thirty-seven dragonfly nymphs ranging from three-eighths to three-quarters of an inch long, deep and thick. The rainbow had in its stomach nearly five hundred midge larvae. This is a sterling example of the different tastes of individual fish.

While I have earnestly tried to describe many nymph fishing methods, I would not want any reader to think that these were the only successful methods, or that other methods should not be used. Do not hesitate to try the unusual and unorthodox; do not accept anyone's word as gospel. I repeat, fish are individuals and have traits and characteristics that are inherent in individuals. Fishermen are individuals also and one should encourage individuality; this is the best method for assuring progress in any field.

I would encourage the nymph gatherer to look seriously at all underwater creatures, not just the ones we have heard so much about. Recently, at the annual meeting of our Southwestern Montana Fly Fishers with Fish and Game representatives, the F & G biologist raised the point that fly-fishermen placed too much emphasis on the may, stone, and caddis imitations and ignored the fact that these make up only a small portion of the total insect supply available to the trout. In the Madison River in Montana, he said, there were *over* a thousand species of underwater forms, yet the may, stone, and caddis composed only about 5 percent of the total, and he urged us to look at the other forms with the idea of imitating them. I agree with him and urge that when you are gathering specimens look closely at all of them.

Trout will sometimes take an artificial nymph in a stretch of stream where the natural never appears. Is this because they may have seen the natural in other locations, and formed a taste for them, or is it perhaps that there are so many kinds of naturals available that the trout become accustomed to taking anything that looks buggy? I favor the latter view, although I haven't a single fact to support it.

If I have made serious nymph fishing appear to be drudgery, it is because I think one cannot take it lightly and still become proficient in its practice. But I enjoy the learning; in the last ten years I have done more observing and studying than I have fishing. During this period I have had the opportunity to study some very advanced anglers—and some very new ones. I have learned some things from both.

In many cases study has just been an excuse to be on the stream. Like Haig-Brown, I do not know if I fish because I like fishing, or if I fish because I love rivers. I do know that I am happier when I am near or in a river and that I could not long exist far from them.

The stream is a book with an endless number of pages; no matter how well one reads or how long, he will always be coming on new and exciting chapters. There is a never-ending fascination beneath the surface of a stream and the happy reader knows that he will never in his lifetime be finished with this lovely book.

Index

Boldface numbers refer to illustrations.